MW00335820

soft
sculpture

soft sculpture

Carolyn Vosburg Hall

left: The First One Here Gets A Box Full of Jello by Barbara Johansen Newman. 18" wide, 15" tall, 10" deep. Soft sculpturing for the joy of it, the artist creates one-of-a-kind characters who involve the viewer in their story. Materials are hand dyed, then embellished with textile paints, hand embroidery, and machine sewn decoration. Photographer, D. Moskowitz. Owner, I. Sigman. Courtesy of the Works Gallery, Philadelphia.

Davis Publications, Inc.
Worcester, Massachusetts

above: Black Man by Lynn DiNino. ¾ scale. "The hip guys hanging out on the street corner late at night inspired this caricature." Added pattern pieces create beautifully modeled lips. Hair assumes a wonderfully abstract shape.

below: Black Man (detail) by Lynn DiNino. Effective forms can result from simple two piece patterns cut carefully. This hand has a wire armature and polyester fiberfill stuffing pushed softly but firmly in place within a knit suede cloth.

Copyright 1981
Davis Publications, Inc.
Worcester, Massachusetts U.S.A.

All rights reserved. No part of this publication may be reproduced or transmitted in any form or by any means, electronic or mechanical, including photocopying, recording, or any storage and retrieval system now known or to be invented, except by a reviewer who wishes to quote brief passages in connection with a review written for inclusion in a magazine, newspaper, or broadcast.

Printed in the United States of America
Library of Congress Catalog Card Number: 80-67546
ISBN: 0-87192-129-4

Composition: Davis Press, Inc.
Type: Souvenir Demi-Bold Display and Sabon Text
Graphic Design: Jean Hodge

10   9   8   7   6   5   4

Cover photo: Two cats from *Nine Cats* series, by the author. Each cat 6″ wide, 12″ long, 15″ high.

Contents

Chapter 1
Introduction

Soft Sculpture is sculpture that is soft. Like "hard" sculpture, it may be three-dimensional and designed to be looked at from more than one angle. Or it may compare to relief sculpture in low dimension and emphasize the textural quality of the fibers used.

Currently, soft sculpture appears in many forms. It may hang in art exhibitions as fine art or it may turn up as toys and play things intended to be fun or nostalgic. Some artists use soft sculpture to make political, poetic, or personal statements. Some treat their materials as color, texture, and line to create fiberforms. Others use the soft plastic quality of fabric like clay. And some paint their soft sculpture.

This diversity makes soft sculpture difficult to define. The ideas and concepts, the aesthetic intentions, the materials, and the uses vary. Soft sculpture began as stitched and stuffed realistic fabric forms, but now is made in a variety of delightful and intuitive ways by people around the country.

History

Claes Oldenburg introduced soft sculpture as a contemporary art form in the 1960s. He constructed super-sized fabric replicas of familiar objects in the manner of the Pop artists. Oldenburg, one of the most inventive American artists, wanted viewers to re-see common objects, which had become so familiar as to be considered invisible. By his unique treatment, he glorified American symbols: the hamburger, the typewriter, the toilet, the fan, or a piece of cake. Roots for this whimsical and outrageous art form can be traced back further to the Dada art movement of the 1920s, in which artists treated ordinary objects in nonsense ways to find new sense. Even longer ago, Victorian stitchers inserted odd little stuffed figures into their embroideries to memorialize friends.

above left: Pug Dog by the author. 12″ wide, 19″ long, 15″ high. (More information on this piece appears in the stuffing section.)

left: Teabag from the series *Four on Plexiglas* (1966) by Claes Oldenburg. 28 1/16″ wide, 39 5/16″ high, 3″ deep. Serigraph printed in red, brown, and silver on felt, clear Plexiglas and white plastic, with felt bag and rayon cord encased. Collection, The Museum of Modern Art, New York. Gift of Lester Avnet.

above: Soft Crackers by Jennifer June. 5½' wide, 1' high, 1' deep. "I wanted to catch that moment at the end of a meal before the clean-up on my studio-cum-lunch table." The super scale immortalizes the ordinary object.

left: Woman Who Lost Her Head by Jennifer June. 4' wide, 8' high, 4' deep. In the classic soft sculpture format invented by Claes Oldenburg, this artist makes a faucet reminiscent of her mother's kitchen in super-sized brightly colored vinyl. She graphically expresses her opinion of women stuck in the backwash of America's kitchens.

Since the sixties, time has been ripe for this art form to flourish and grow. Mariska Karask had already diminished objections to stitchery appearing as art work. In the 1950s, she embroidered wall hangings with relaxed and expanded stitches that flowed like painted lines. She designed her stitcheries as painters do rather than follow the strict controls that traditional embroidery required. She completed the move from craft to art by framing her works, realizing that people were more apt to consider framed work art. Art today is so diverse and multi-directional that the artificial lines dividing the "fine arts" from "crafts" have little meaning. Paintings have become three-dimensional. Sculptors paint their works. Both use craft materials. Potters make non-useful pots. Weavers disregard flat yardage in favor of three-dimensional fiberworks. And people everywhere are making soft sculpture.

With all these changes, it is not easy to evaluate contemporary art works. As a useful guideline, learn to measure these works by their own standards. Examine each piece carefully to determine what it intends to say or be, and how successfully it accomplishes these ends.

above left: Pectens by Suzi Johnson. 16″ wide, 19″ high, 29″ long. This soft scallop shell displays a variety of techniques: a photo silk-screened design printed with procion dyes on cotton sateen; quilting stitches and trapunto stuffing for a bas-relief surface and stronger form; aluminum armature for support; and beading and embroidery for embellishment.

right: Untitled by Jean Battles-Irvin. 40″ wide, 60″ high, 1″ deep. This shrine-like piece combines macrame, crochet, wrapping, stuffing, drawing, machine knitting and fine craftsmanship harmoniously. Materials include wool, beads, buttons, paper, satin, cotton, ivory, and polyester fiberfill. Photographer, Stan T. Irvin.

below: Nellapelliona (detail) by Becky Clark. 48″ wide, 48″ tall, 4″ deep. This study in repetition of simple shapes is knotted with half-hitches in bleached and natural jute cord. The macrame knots construct a firm sculptural form. Photographer, Jeffrey Clark.

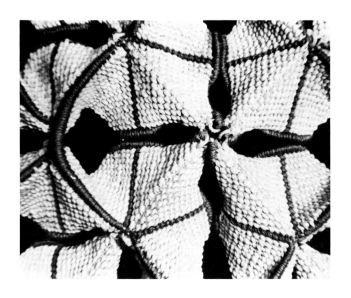

Soft Sculpture Today

Soft sculpture has enormous appeal to viewers and artists alike. Since it is still a new medium there are plenty of surprises left. Artists like the wide range of concepts and techniques available to them. Both artists and viewers constantly come in contact with fiber and fabrics in their lives, thereby having a ready knowledge and appreciation of textile qualities.

The materials and tools used to make soft sculpture are available everywhere and are easy to use. Fabrics and yarns can be bought in a vast variety of textures, colors, weights, and costs. A search in the closet or scrap bag may turn up useful fabrics. These materials can be worked into shape by common means: sewing, weaving, crocheting, embroidering, and other techniques easy to learn.

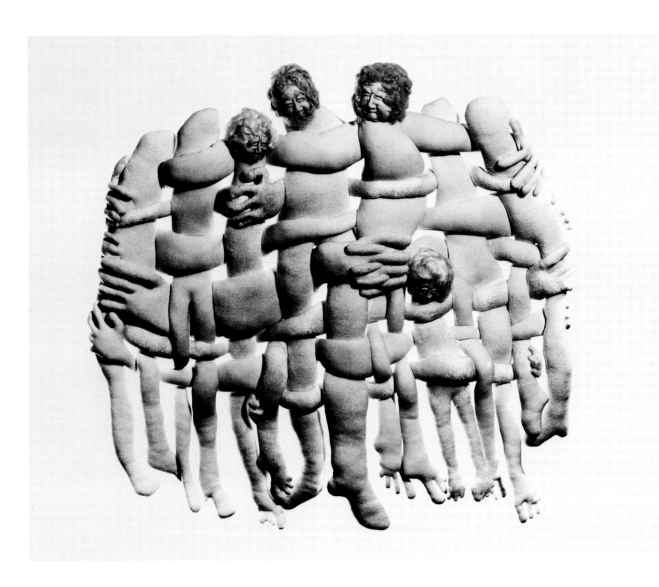

above: Closely Woven Family by Marjorie Trout. 33″ wide, 31″ high, 7″ deep. The artist uses soft sculpture as a vehicle for social commentary, combining the cohesiveness of the family with her views of life as a weaving teacher. Photographer, Bucher & Young.

Ideas

Thought waves seem to float in the air causing people in various parts of the country to pop up with identical images simultaneously. Soft sculpture artists get ideas from everything around them and from developing their own concepts and experiments. Ideas lead to new ideas.

Soft sculpture as an art form grows and changes, fed by the continuing contributions of artists in the field. Traditions have developed, based largely on the imagery and concepts of people like Claes Oldenburg. We all share these ideas, acknowledging their value and then altering or expanding on them in our own ways. This book presents many innovative soft sculpture projects and will trigger your imagination.

above right: Blue Fairy by Barbara Johansen Newman. 15" wide, 36" tall, 10" deep. Hand dyed fabrics are embroidered and sewn into shape, then stuffed firmly over an armature to create this very real little person with sharp elbows, plump thighs, and a snappy gesture. Her delightful, carefully hand stitched face invites the viewer to join the party. Photographer, Harvey Ferdschneider. Courtesy of the Works Gallery, Philadelphia.

above left: Irene Weaves by the author. 15" wide, 18" high, 4" deep. This portrait pillow, made for my editor (Van Nostrand Reinhold — *The Sewing Machine Crafts Book*) shows her with laced fingers to demonstrate the "tabby" weave. Marjorie Trout's image and mine both interweave human forms and are a visual play on the word weave. Our works occurred simultaneously but we had no knowledge of each other.

below: Man Emerging by Christine Carpenter. 20" wide, 31" high, 5" deep. The struggling soft form emerging from the sharp edged shapes expresses the interaction between two opposing forces. The artist uses this relationship to suggest philosophic meaning. Photographer, Jeff Newberry.

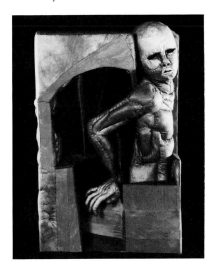

Goal

The examples, diagrams, and instructions included can help turn good ideas into realities. In addition to information about stuffings, fibers, and fabrics, armatures, construction, and surface design techniques, two special sections are included. Chapter six gives specific information on how to make accurate patterns from a sketch. Most soft sculptors construct their figures intuitively, cutting and fitting to achieve the right shapes. My measure-and-math technique diminishes guess work and speeds pattern making.

Chapter two demystifies the design process — as much as one can with a creative activity. Analysis of the way professional designers develop an idea into an object resulted in a design check list. You can try this list on a new idea or an unfinished piece to help make the necessary decisions.

Why do people make soft sculpture? Art may be important for its serious subject matter, complex color relationships, heroic size, or enduring materials. However, soft sculpture often flies in the face of such ponderous preferences and exists for sheer joy, whimsy, or expression of love.

Chapter 2
Design by Decision

People commonly ask artists where they get their ideas. Active artists say ideas grow out of their experiences like new leaves on trees. Anything can germinate a new idea. To find ideas, look at any book, exhibition, magazine, or even TV show that offers a new experience. Look at the way nature creates beauty with structural logic. Examine feelings, and explore every new idea from several points of view. Ideas can come in many ways and from anywhere.

The ability to change the idea into an object seems a bit magical. Almost anybody can dream up images, but embodying them in aesthetic form takes skill and practice. The most exuberant people grab materials and whack them into shape by trial and error. Soft sculptures made this way have a charming spontaneity. They also might have bursting seams and floppy necks. It helps to plan ahead.

Design Principles

Design principles developed to help analyze and plan a project. These principles, rules, and concepts grew out of the creative process. Some can be learned before working but most are discovered while creating.

Experienced artists agree that a problem halting construction of an art work is an unmade decision or a wrong direction. In changing idea into object you must consider size, color, technique, purpose, and other factors. Designing is thus a decisionmaking process and an investigation of how to best integrate concepts with materials.

Design can be broken into many facets. Elements of design flow through all art. Lines, shapes, and volumes are the basic units. An artist learns to arrange them in assorted ways to achieve different effects. *Repetition* of similar shapes or colors makes them more important, creates flow, and develops rhythm. *Contrast* adds spice to the sweetness of harmony. It comes from sharp differences in colors, textures, shapes, sizes, or materials. *Variation* provides interest by mixing different shapes or forms, such as curved with angular, thick with thin.

left: Topiary Tree (detail)

above left: Yankee Pot Roast by Joann Chaney. 3′ wide, 3′ deep, 2′ high. Intimate knowledge of cooking guided this artist in dye painting, cutting patterns, and constructing an oversized casserole.

above right: Auto Bon-Bon by Diane Spring Slade. 12″ wide, 12″ long, 12″ high. Recalling her adolescent fascination with machines, especially the "convertible," the artist reconstructs an exquisite miniature car with deep purple velvet body, silver lamé chrome, red satin tail lights, stretch terry cloth seats, and silver thread for tiny details. The car replaces cupid on a white velvet valentine box.

above: Containers II by Ann McKenzie Nicholson. 8½″ wide, 11″ high, 2″ deep. A simple geometric form, carefully wrapped in subtly dyed strips of silk, becomes a row of intriguing packages that are "not functional containers, but are about containers." Ideas need not be complex or elaborately handled to be effective.

Lines, shapes, and volumes, altered by these principles of organization (as well as by color and texture), have different impacts. The *movement*, the way your eyes move when viewing an art work, can vary considerably. Forms or colors may be repeated *rhythmically* with varied intervals for enrichment. Or one special shape, color, or texture may receive *emphasis*, commanding attention like the clash of cymbals in music. The overall design of a soft sculpture may be symmetrical like a church tower or dramatically asymmetrical like a Japanese bonsai tree. Whatever final effect, you will sense the visual stability or *balance* of a form in space.

Harmony, another design consideration, results when all aspects of a work are congruent and well integrated. No single element jars the whole. *Proportion,* the logical relationship among all components, is one aspect of harmony.

Keep these concepts in mind when you create, evaluate a work, or complete a checklist as described in the next section.

above: Nine Cats by the author. Each cat 6" wide, 12" long, 15" high. Five of the nine cats show variations on the basic form. The surface treatment catches the character of various well remembered cats by embroidery, tie dye, varied colors, exposed stuffing through a transparent mylar, and even a grass covered framework for the cat who loved stalking outside.

right: Lida Gordon duplicates the soft container twelve times, de-emphasizing its uniqueness. She groups the balls into a larger circle to repeat and emphasize their roundness.

below: Soft Containers by Lida Gordon. Each container about 12" around. Multiple units allow for variations on a theme showing changing relationships. The basic unit has shirred satin sides wrapped enticingly around clusters of hand sewn French knots.

above: Three Graces by Mary Jane Mazucowski. 10" wide, 18" tall, 4" thick. Technique affects the choice of materials. Batik requires good quality natural fiber fabric to accept dyes well. Embroidered figures might well be smaller. Knitted figures would need a simplified graphed pattern to suit the knit stitch. The simple outline shape allows the batik dyed figures to carry the design message.

below: Uncle Sam Hat by Scott Nelles. 15" × 15" × 15". The carved, sewn, and painted leather hat makes a patriotic statement. Nelles conceived the hat as a symbol of the U.S.A., durable, venerable, appealing, and somewhat snappy in style.

Design Checklist

The accompanying checklist for making soft sculpture simplifies design into a manageable system. The list can be used to plan a piece and to anticipate or solve problems. Each factor in the list will now be discussed.

Checklist for Designing Soft Sculpture

Begin with any factor, write in your decision. Fill in other spaces and cross check to see how decisions affect one another. Keep the elements of design in mind for all choices.

Factors	Decisions
TECHNIQUE	
IDEA	
PURPOSE/FUNCTION	
FORM	
COLOR RANGE	
MATERIALS	
SIZE	
COST/TIME	
CONSISTENCY	
OTHER	

above: Great White Wave by Jennifer June. 23′ wide, 15′ high, 3′ deep. This artist comments upon woman and her place in society in an unexpected way.

below: Untitled by Kathryn McCardle Lipke. 30″ wide, 40″ high, 4″ deep. Successful forms result from careful selections and arrangement of the components. Round, naturalistic shapes grow into tubular shapes with rhythmic flow. Randomly varied widths and loops echo these forms and contribute new ones.

TECHNIQUE

The means used to make an art work is called the technique. Soft sculpture employs any number of fiber techniques, such as fabric construction, knitting, knotting, macrame, batik, embroidery, weaving, or quilting. Choosing technique first exerts strong influence on other choices. For instance, batik technique affects choice of materials. Embroidery influences time, size, or both. The detail in knitted or crocheted figures requires simplified graphed designs. The choice of technique limits what you can do. These limitations define like fences, corraling your ideas into manageable form.

IDEA

Idea is the central theme of an art work. Writers express concepts in words, artists state them in visual images. The "Conceptual Art" movement blossomed during the last decade. At its zenith, a Chicago exhibition required artists only to mail or phone in their concepts for display. Viewers could read them and deal mind to mind with the artist, no need for the actual work.

But people love art for more than the pure idea. They love colors and shapes, the feel of the materials, and the story told. They like to see, touch, and own it. Just as people need bodies to contain their brains, art needs substance and form to contain ideas.

Not all ideas are lofty and complex. Many are neat and simple. It only matters that the form fit the idea. The idea helps define the art work, giving a guide for making decisions.

PURPOSE/FUNCTION

Some artists recognize their purpose before they begin a project; others discover it as they create. You may not know why you feel compelled to make art. Your subconscious often supplies you with reasons and your intuitive motivation gives force to these ideas. The final piece often projects these feelings for others to share.

To define function, ask yourself how the piece will be used: Is it to play with, to express an idea, to sit on, to enter in a show, to wear, to stand on a pedestal? Pieces for exhibition, expression, or enjoyment are most often shaped by aesthetic standards and intuitive motivation. Artists designing pieces to sit on, wear, or for play must consider strength, durability, comfort, and other functional factors in addition to aesthetic standards. "Form follows function" means that purpose predicts structure, and structure affects form.

Design by Decision   17

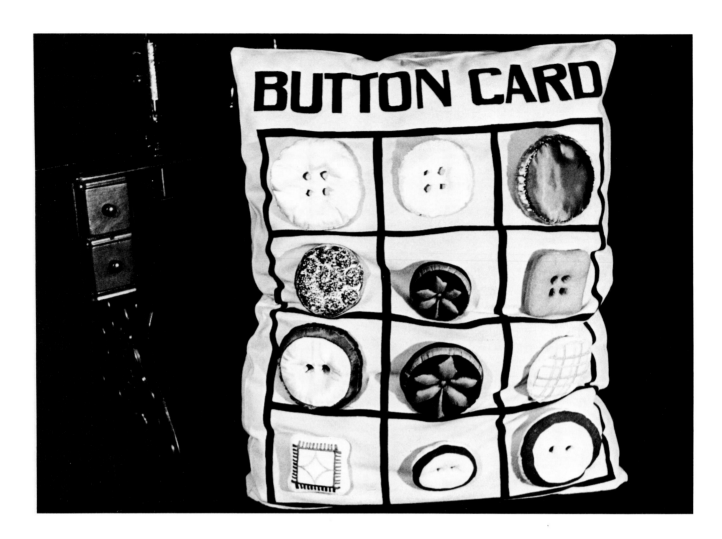

above: Button Card by Julie Staller Pentalnik. 32″ wide, 45″ high, 7″ deep. Finding just the right button can assume enormous importance. Making an ordinary object super-sized draws attention to it. Often visual puns are implied. Photographer, Dan Korn.

FORM

Form is the space an object fills whether real or implied. Sculpture has three-dimensional form while drawings simply imply dimension. Artists have learned to arrange the component parts of an art work to lead the viewer to see relationships, images, directions, meaning, and implications. For example, the artist may repeat round or linear shapes, vary them in size and placement, emphasize some with color, and harmonize the whole with related textures.

Soft sculpture requires a form that supports itself in space. This form is structure, the underlying bones of a piece. Form results directly from construction and design.

COLOR

Color is emotion. It can cheer, calm, delight, overwhelm, or intrigue. Colors depict mood and feeling. They can be bright for happiness, muted for serenity, intense for

anger, or dark for sorrow. But perhaps you see anger as dark, sorrow as gray, or serenity as clear. Color expresses your feelings in art in a wonderfully personal way.

Colors exist in relationship to each other. Gray is lighter than black, darker than white. Calm blue, next to its opposite orange, jiggles your eyes. (The Op artists of the 1960s exploited this phenomenon in their high keyed hard edge art.) Examine how colors appear in nature. A yellow crocus shines brightly amid drab March but is dim compared to June's brilliant orange poppies. Not all colors need contrast. The tweedy brown toad camouflages himself on matching soil.

In the language of color notation: *hue* names a color, red, yellow, or blue; *value* measures the light or darkness of hue; and, *chroma* indicates the intensity or muted quality of a color.

Almost everyone has an inborn color sense. You, as an artist, may well perceive color better than most, just as a musician hears music more perceptively. To develop your color sense study color theory and practice using colors. When analyzing a piece, consider various combinations to find the most effective for expressing your feeling.

MATERIALS

If color is emotion, then materials are the sensual element of art. They offer two rich sources for effect. In your art, check to see if the materials enhance the design. Consider how the materials handle; are they heavy, flimsy, stretchy or prickly? Can you make them do your bidding? What is the most effective way to use them? Many fabrics, for example, project traditional imagery. Satin is sleek, burlap crude, brocade rich, and gray flannel business-like. Make these images work for you or use deliberate contrasts to create excitement.

SIZE/SCALE

Increased size demands attention. Reduced size may add intimacy. Life-size implies reality. Size may be chosen for the following reasons: to accommodate materials, to suit construction technique, to fit somewhere, to increase importance, or to save cost.

Experiment with different sizes to see how you work best. Some people revel in the intimacy of tiny works while others require larger scope to swing into a project.

COST/TIME

Estimate how much the materials you would like to use will cost. If it seems too much, can you reduce the size, change to another material, recycle something in your closet, or shop at the sales? Estimate how much time the

above: 8 Pack by Dee Durkee. Life-sized. Minimal materials and a discarded container made this appealing soft sculpture. The artist hand painted these firmly stuffed bottles but now screen prints some pieces to save time.

below: BFD 1000, Clockwatcher series by Eileen DeRosa Patra. 26″ wide, 10″ tall, 15″ deep. As a personal comment on the secretarial world, the artist turns down the corners of the typewriter like a drooping mouth. Exaggerated shapes contribute to the overall meaning.

project might take. Can you afford the time, make it smaller or simpler, figure out ways to speed some techniques, or get help from friends? Good art works rarely result from poor materials. Further, your time is worth money. Let's add to the old saying, "Anything worth doing is worth doing well . . . and with good quality materials."

CONSISTENCY

Ask yourself, "How well do the component parts of this piece fit the whole art work? Are all parts equally stylized? (It is hard to make a realistic face look right on an abstract body.) Does the technique suit the form? Do the materials give the same message as the forms they cover? Are all proportions in scale?" Consistency is harmony however you achieve it.

OTHER FACTORS

Other considerations important to your work might be message, care, fit, appeal to buyers, or requirements for an exhibition. Add factors to your list until you have covered necessary points. Once you know how to control design factors, you will be able to visualize an object and have it turn out as expected. A very heady feeling comes when you gain control. Then you can begin to "break the rules," aim for intentional inconsistencies, experiment with sizes, combine colors in unusual ways, or exaggerate shapes for heightened effects.

To see how the design checklist works, glance through my decisions listed in approximate order for planning the *Topiary Tree.* Now select a piece you are planning and fill out the list. Start in any order. With one decision made, you will be able to confront the others more comfortably. With luck you may be able to decide everything first and work from start to finish. If you cannot make all decisions or do not have time to resolve them, begin by making the ones you can and cope with the others as you come to them.

Experienced artists sometimes start pieces incompletely planned. They gamble that problems they encounter will force fresh, imaginative solutions. A good art work looks so consistent and right, it is hard to believe the artist worked diligently to bring all the parts into harmony.

Some factors on the checklist will relate more to your piece than to others. If points you need are not listed, add them. You may wish to make several copies of the list for other projects. Eventually, design by decision becomes so automatic that you do it in your head.

Topiary Tree by the author.

Design checklist for *Topiary Tree*

Factors	Decision
TECHNIQUE	First decision made. I want to try the slit back trapunto technique. This requires a surface pattern to stitch, so I plan to dye paint the design. Dyes keep the fabric surface softer than paint.
IDEA	Next, why not make a formal topiary tree with a cluster of tiny leaves to stitch around for stuffing? I can begin to see an image in my mind. From here on, I seem to describe my imagined tree more than make intellectual choices.
PURPOSE/ FUNCTION	My practical goal is to make an exhibition piece. In addition, we all have secret purposes in making art — to capture and portray the essence of our subjects and to express deep felt emotions and ideas. I love and need trees.
FORM	A square tree with flat sides will allow me to work on trapunto stuffing and to cope with fewer seams. A wooden "T" shaped frame could support the tree. Perhaps a mound of grass should cover the base?
COLOR RANGE	Easy. Trees are green. I will save breaking that tradition for another piece. Touches of orange-red and dark-green can highlight the olive-green leaves and grass. I can't miss on the trunk color if I combine orange and olive-green to make a warm ochre-brown.
MATERIALS	Influenced by technique, I need a fabric that accepts good dye color, and stitches and quilts well. A machine-turned post from the lumber yard makes a good tree trunk.
SIZE	Size develops from purpose, technique, and materials. Not so large as to take forever and not too small to work on. The tree trunk size determines proportions. Stability requirements affect the size and shape of the base.
COST/TIME	Since I have most materials on hand, cost is small. Without a well stocked studio or scrap pile, expenses could be a major consideration. Time causes changes. Hand stitching the leaves takes too long so I will machine sew the rest. Regular machine stitching is cumbersome so I will use the free motion sewing machine technique (chapter 8 — machine embroidery).
CONSISTENCY	I want the leaves to have the same simple geometry as the trunk, the color to express the idea, and the trapunto technique to suit the shape of the tree.

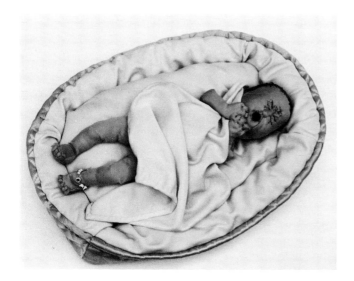

Newborn by Lois Bro. 24" long. The artist's close, careful study of her subject produces a sensitive, authentic portrait of a baby's first exciting hours.

Beginning a Project

If you cannot make all your design choices at once, begin one step at a time. Copy a well made soft sculpture or use a printed pattern. From this you gain experience in construction and a feeling for materials by working with them.

Next, make a change. Change the colors. All those people flipping through the pattern books at the fabric store are making decisions about colors and textures. You have made similar choices.

When you see this change succeed, try another. Change the shape of the pattern or the size. Proceed at your own pace, learning as you go. The more decisions you make, coupled with your added skill in construction, the easier decisions become. Not all ideas need be startlingly new. Many are variations or new combinations of existing ideas. Apply the design checklist to other people's works to see how they accomplished their results. Now look around for ideas with your educated eye. You are ready to design your own soft sculpture.

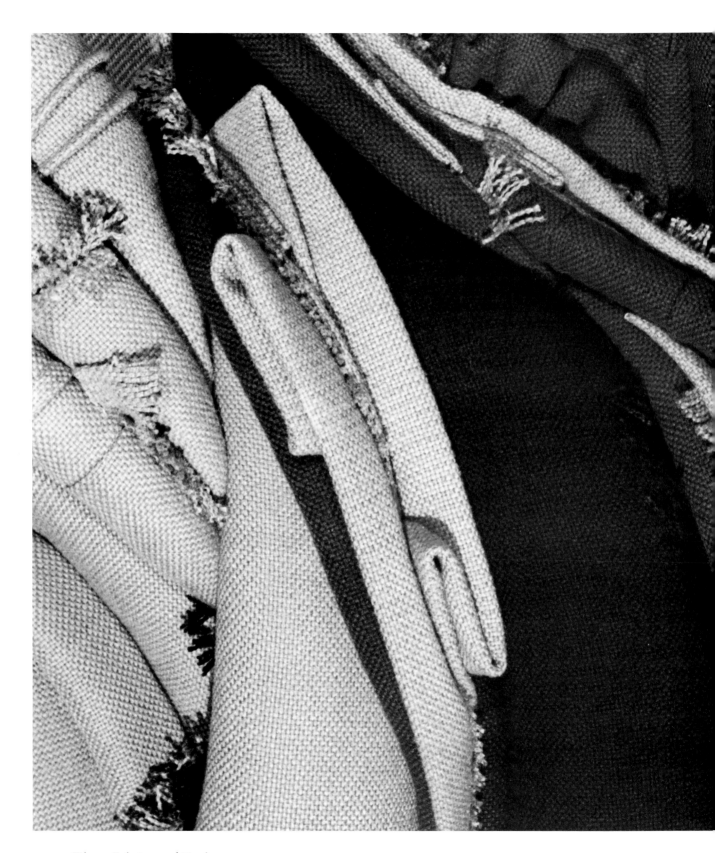

Fibers, Fabrics, and Tools

Chapter 3
Fibers, Fabrics, and Tools

The form, style, and technique of soft sculptures grow from the basic nature of materials and the way you use them. It is easier to visualize and construct a piece if you understand how fibers and fabrics handle. Knowledge gained from this experience aids in choosing the right materials for desired effects.

Fibers and fabrics are softer than a sculptor's stone and sturdier than a printmaker's paper. A good fabric can take a lot of reworking and still hold up well. You can sculpt, fold, drape, dye, stretch, gather, seam, cut, or paint on it.

Rosalie Sherman's attitude is like most soft sculptors': "I like a variety of materials, but fabric really appeals to me. I can make a large volume with the least amount of weight. I also like the range of colors and textures, and how various fabrics reflect and absorb light. Fabric is very skin-like."

For most soft sculptors, fibers and fabrics are not only convenient and easy to use but essential to expressing their ideas. Some use fabric as a characterless basic material for creating forms as the sculptor uses clay. Others love the color and texture of the fibers themselves and emphasize the surface design created by manipulating fibers.

Fibers

Fabrics, yarns, and cords are all made from fibers. By definition, a fiber must be at least 100 times as long as it is wide to have the necessary flexibility to spin or weave. In addition to length, strength, and flexibility, good textile fibers may have other useful characteristics such as: fiber shape, uniformity, density, luster, moisture absorbency, elasticity, resilience, and resistance to damage. These qualities affect weight, sheen, appearance, wear, and comfort of fabrics.

left: Detail of wall hanging by Robert Kidd. The nature of the fabrics suggests ways to be used, with shadowy sharp folds, diagonal folds for flexibility, and frayed edges that reveal the fibers still crimped by the weave.

above: Wings by Rosalie Sherman. 112″ wide, 27″ tall, 9″ thick. Nylon fabric stretched with grommets, snaps, and D-rings on a carved cherry wood frame create this fantasy equipment "relic of another culture, familiar as in dreams."

below: Untitled by Robert Kidd. 4′ wide, 4′ high, 8″ deep. This wall sculpture consists of a rich assortment of fabrics, draped in a natural flow, then firmly stuffed and attached to a rigid backing. Machine sewn tucks counterpoint the sweep of plain fabric.

Textile fibers come from a variety of sources. Some exist in nature virtually ready to use: cotton comes from a plant; wool from animal hairs, especially sheeps'; and silk from silkworms. Other fibers are artificially made but include plant substances: rayon is made from wood cellulose and spandex from rubber. Synthetics are also made from minerals — fiberglass from sand and polyester from petroleum.

Natural fibers grow in short lengths called staple, which are spun into threads, yarns, or cords. Synthetic fibers result from reducing raw materials to a syrup, then forcing it through a spinnaret machine. Like spaghetti, out comes a continuous monofilament strand. Filament cords or yarns, such as monofilament fish line and nylon cord, are smooth and strong.

Synthetic fibers may lack the qualities of natural ones but technology can improve them. Staple cut acrylic is lighter and loftier (fluffy, non-compacted) than wool. Crimped polyester becomes stretchy. Expanded fibers become more absorbent. Shaping fibers round, flat, or rough alters luster and appearance. Added chemicals affect flammability, dyeing, and absorbency. Similar processes can alter and improve natural fibers as well. For example, mercerizing cotton strengthens the fiber and adds luster.

Crinkly fibers twisted loosely into yarns make lofty textured yarns. Tighter spinning and twisting adds strength. Combinations of natural and synthetic yarns can result in the best qualities of both.

above: Fred by Jill Frey. 18″ wide, 18″ high, 18″ long. Frey uses natural cotton and plain tabby weave to "clothe" the stuffed sculptured forms of this invented creature.

right: Mask by Joan Berke. 15″ wide, 24″ high, 4″ deep. Raffia, rough fibers, and wools add to the mysterious character of primitive masks. This loom woven piece is embellished with wrapping, braiding, and other hand applied touches.

below: Beauty is More than Skin Deep by Rosalie Shirley. 23″ in diameter, 5″ tall. "People *are* beautiful inside. I had to show an elegant soul in an interesting exterior." The homely crocheted jute and sisal freestanding fiber sculpture contains a silk embroidered soul done in Igolochkoy, a Russian miniature punch needle technique. Photographer, Ken Heywood.

FIBER CHART

NATURAL PLANT FIBERS

Cotton   grows as fluffy white puffs in seed pods. The world's most common fiber, cotton fibers are strong, crinkly, absorbent, spin well, and dye readily. Among its many uses: threads, cords, yarns, ropes, battings, paper, and all weights and weaves of fabric. It may shrink, wrinkle, or mildew in prolonged dampness.

Linen   is derived from the stem of flax plants. Linen fibers are very strong, absorb well, have a natural luster, dye well, and do not stretch. It may shrink, wrinkle, mildew, or crock (dye rubs off).

Jute, Hemp, Sisal   are inexpensive, rough textured, "natural" colored fibers with little stretch and flexibility. Jute (used as cord or burlap) loses strength by decomposition. To prevent this, immerse it in a solution of swimming pool algaecide to create a fatty film coating which prevents bacteria or fungus growth.

NATURAL ANIMAL FIBERS

Wool   can be shorn from many animals: among them, sheep, goats (mohair), camels, and llamas. Wool fibers are crinkly in shape, scaley in microscopic detail, and resilient. Because of these qualities wool spins beautifully, stretches, resumes its shape, and remains lofty. It molds well when pressed and felts naturally when heat, moisture, and pressure are applied. Wool dyes well. It can shrink, attract moths, weaken from sun.

Silk   unwinds in a continuous tiny filament from silk worm cocoons. It has deep luster, super strength for its size, good elasticity, and dyes beautifully. Silk may waterspot or deteriorate from high heat.

SYNTHETIC FIBERS

Rayon   made from wood cellulose, dyes like other plant fibers and can resemble natural fibers. Rayon is soft, drapes well, dyes to rich colors, absorbs well, and washes easily. It may shrink and has little strength.

Acetate   has a rich, silk-like sheen. It resists shrinking and stretching, absorbs little, and dries quickly. It may wrinkle and wear when rubbed. Combined rayon and acetate achieve the best qualities of both.

Polyester   is very strong, non-absorbent (dries rapidly), requires complex chemistry to dye, and does not wrinkle. Combined with cotton or wool it cuts shrinkage, wrinkles, and absorbency. Versatile polyester is used for clothing, fabrics, curtains, strong threads, rope, tire cording, stuffing, and more.

Acrylic   has softness, resilience, and bulk without weight. It holds its shape well, resists wrinkles, dries quickly, but may pill. It is used for blankets, fur fabrics, sweaters, knit fabrics, and wool-like fabrics.

Modacrylic   is soft, fleecy, and resilient. It is moth and mildew proof, dries fast, resists wrinkles, but is very heat sensitive. Used for wigs.

Nylon   the strongest fiber of all is elastic, abrasion resistant, smooth, resilient, lustrous, and low in absorbency. It combines well with other fibers and appears in many weaves and textures.

Olefin   the lightest of synthetic fibers, has the same qualities as other synthetics. In addition it has high bulk without weight and it is good for carpeting, knits, pile, and upholstery fabrics.

Fiberglass   a mineral fiber, is strong, fireproof, and will not fade. It breaks when sharply bent. Used for drapery and resin reinforcement in boats and sculpture.

Metallic   fibers must be blended with other fibers for strength. Plastic coated metallic fibers will not tarnish.

Spandex   a very elastic rubber fiber, is combined with other fibers for stretchy fabrics. It cannot stand much heat.

above: *A Persuasion of Pleats* by B. J. Adams. 18″ wide, 14″ high, 1″ deep. Knife edged pleats carefully ironed into striped silk fabric builds a texture that reveals the lustrous silk colors. Hidden stitching in the grooves hold the sculptured silk to a velveteen background. Photographer, Clark G. Adams.

below: *Gauze Book* by Sas Colby. 8″ wide by 8″ high. This hand-stitched book of mixed fabrics features the log cabin quilt pattern to frame printed fabric designs, suggesting an ancient textile.

above: *Water Lily* by Lou Souders. 14″ wide, 8″ deep. Aiming to portray the delicate beauty of a transient flower, white satin was chosen for petals (stiffened with pellon), yellow rayon fringe for stamens, and green satin for the lily pad.

Fabrics

Fabrics result from fibers intermeshed by weaving, knitting, crocheting, felting, knotting, tatting, netting, or other means of assembly. The construction of a fabric affects how it will handle, cut, stitch by hand or machine, hold its shape, stretch, dye, fray on the edges, or hold firm seams.

In addition, the fiber content, type of yarns, and finishes all impart characteristics to fabrics. Nothing tells you more about a fabric than its look and feel. To test a fabric: fold it (for thickness of multiple seams), drape it, stretch it (too much? too little?), scratch it with your fingernail (to test for sizing), rub it (to test dye fastness), wad it (for resilience), and read the tag on storebought fabrics. Also check the entire piece of fabric you plan to buy for misweaves or poor dyeing. Try sewing a sample to see if you can achieve the results you want.

FINISHES

Common permanent finishes that alter and improve fabrics include: "beetling" or pounding the fabric to flatten and fill the weave and impart luster; "calendaring" or running the fabric over hot rollers for a smooth finish; "fulling" of wool by applying heat, moisture, and pressure to compact the weave, add body, and stability; "mercerization" to improve the beauty, durability, and dyeing of cotton; and "napping" to raise short ends of spun yarns on the fabric surface by brushing. Many synthetic fabrics are heat sealed after knitting or weaving for dimensional stability.

Sizing gives a temporary finish (starch, gum, wax) that improves body, weight, and luster. Wash out sizings before you dye or paint a fabric. Fabrics listed by finish on their hang tags as crease resistant, wash and wear, or water repellent will also resist dyeing or painting.

Fabric Grain

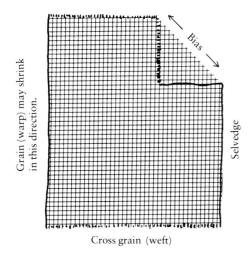

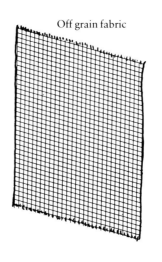

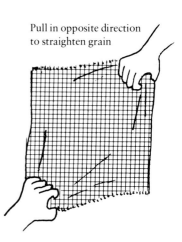

above: Sitting Pretty by Ann Watson. 15″ wide, 18″ high, 15″ deep. Look how seriously this stitched and stuffed lady takes displaying her assortment of fabrics; machine woven lace, tapestry woven upholstery, spun wool hair, and various other cottons, satins, and synthetics. Her lips curve in a Mona-Lisa embroidered smile. Photographer, Joe Watson.

GRAIN

With woven fabrics "grain" refers to the firm, strong warp threads running the length of a fabric. "Crossgrain" applies to the weft or filler threads woven across the warp. These may stretch more than the grain. "Bias" refers to a diagonal line or cut across fabric that will stretch or gather easily. You can take advantage of these characteristics by placing pattern pieces carefully on the fabric. Some fabrics are pulled off-grain at the mill. Steam, press, or pull in the opposite direction to correct this problem. Some poorly printed and some bonded fabrics are fixed permanently off-grain.

CHARACTER

Soft sculptors care more about color, texture, strength, and workability when choosing fabrics than about shrinkage, wear, or warmth. They like muslin because of its firm weave, off-white color, and low cost. They like suede cloth, velveteen, and satin because of their rich surfaces. They like the stretch of knits, the non-fraying character of felt, or the translucency of chiffon. For starters, use one fabric until you know it well. But sometimes you need a special quality for a certain effect. The fabric chart lists them by characteristic to help you choose.

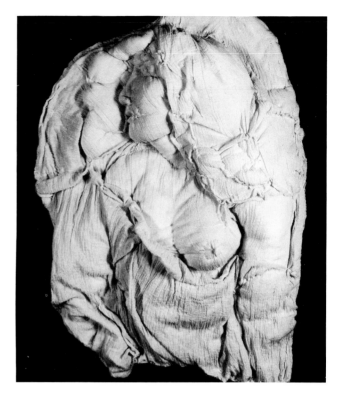

right: Mid Summer Night by Constance McCardle. 24″ wide, 34″ high. "This piece created itself." Working from a strong inner vision, the artist modeled 6 yards of uncut ecru cotton muslin over batting into a sleeping figure.

below left: Nude in a "G" String by Barbara Johansen Newman. 15″ wide, 15″ high, 4″ deep. "Stretch" says this acrobatic pose, clearly demonstrating the "stretch in every direction" characteristics of single knit fabrics. Photographer, Harvey Ferdschneider.

below right: Woman in Boots by Barbara Johansen Newman. 10″ wide, 18″ high, 8″ deep. The expandable knit undershirt, the squiggly machine embroidered belt, the pleated fabric skirt, and the painted boots combine to make a lively caricature.

Fibers, Fabrics, and Tools   29

FABRIC CHART (CHOICE BY CHARACTERISTICS)

Plain weave, medium weight
Plain or tabby weave means every yarn is overlaced with every other yarn. The closer the weave the more dimensional stability. The firmer the yarn the firmer the fabric. Finishes also firm fabrics.

Balloon cloth (cotton, silk, rayon, or nylon), calico, muslin or cambric (usually cotton, starched or sized), chambray (white warp, colored weft gives frosted look, cotton), chintz (glazed cotton), gingham (woven plaid or check), denim (twill weave), long-cloth, broadcloth, percale (some luster), muslin (shrinks), madras (woven plaid, colors run), Oxford cloth (basket weave), scrim (open weave). These fabrics are usually made from cotton or cotton plus polyester.

Plain weave, sheer and light weight
Woven fabrics made with fine yarns (threads), loosely packed are sheer. Soft yarns with no finishes make soft and drapey fabrics.

Albatross (pebbly surface, crepe yarns), bunting (flags and banners, cotton or wool), casement cloth (curtains, synthetics), challis (cotton, wool, other), chiffon (silk, wool, synthetic), crepe de chine (silk or synthetic), Georgette (filmy), cashmere, Surrah (soft twill) silk challis.

Crisp, stiff light to medium weight
Stiffness comes from tightly packed weaving, stiff or treated fibers, added finishes, or construction (felting or laminating).

Bengaline (ribbed weave), brilliantine (woven, soft or stiff), brocatelle (raised design), jaquard weave (medium to heavy), buchram (used for stiffening), crinolin (sized for stiffness), dimity (sheer, light), ninon (thin, smooth, crisp), tailor's canvas (stiff hairs woven in), organdy (thin, smooth, crisp), sharkskin (sleek, hard finish, synthetic or wool), tarlatan (light, open, stiffened).

Firmly woven
Threads tightly packed or large yarns packed many to the inch result in firm weaving. Plain or twill weave may be used.

Bengaline (fine covering warp, heavy weft), Byrd cloth (light weight, tight weave, wind resistant), cavalry twill (medium to heavy), faille (soft, firm, ribbed), covert (wool or cotton twill, medium to heavy), gabardine (twill, medium to heavy), grosgrain (heavy rib, used for ribbon), taffeta (stiff, lustrous), ticking (many weaves, for bedding, firm weave to keep feathers in).

Firmly woven, heavy
Heavy yarns tightly packed make heavy fabrics.

Art linen (soft to firm, light to heavy for embroidery), awning, duck, canvas (plain weave, medium to heavy), bedford cord (firm twill), covert, denim, frisé (coarse, heavy, napped twill), muslin, tweed (variegated wool), sailcloth.

Pile, napped (brushed) or furry
Pile surface results from: brushing up yarn ends, weaving a looped thread (terrycloth). Double weave looped and then sheared (velvet), applied flock fibers adhered to backing (suede cloth), or softly spun furry yarns brushed.

Alpaca (soft, lustrous brushed wool), broadcloth ("fulled", napped, sheared), camel's hair (wool fulled [felted] brushed), cashmere (soft wool), chenille (furry, cut pile yarns), chinchilla (wool or cotton, curled tufts), corduroy (sheared pile in ribs), duvetyn (soft, silky, brushed), sueded cotton (brushed), flannel (cotton or wool brushed), flannelette (cotton brushed), mackinaw cloth (plaid wool, compacted brushed), mohair (angora goat wool, compacted brushed), melton (lustrous wool, compacted brushed), velvet (lustrous sheared pile), velveteen (low luster cotton, sheered pile), terry (cotton loops weave), velour (soft, brushed), suede cloth (applied flock fibers).

Lustrous
Satin weave or shiny fibers. The satin weave has long overshots so natural sheen of the fiber shows.

Glazed chintz, crepe (shiny fibers, pebbly yarn), doeskin (soft brushed leather look), lamé (metallic threads), peau de soie ("silk skin"), satin, sateen (satin weave, mercerized cotton).

Elaborate weaves
Plaids and stripes result from weaving colored threads. Dimensional weaves come from a programmed loom that interlaced threads in a set pattern. These looms are called dobby, jaquard leno, or malmo depending upon how they work.

Birds eye (diamond weave cotton), brocade (rich raised design, jaquard loom weave), brocatelle (raised jaquard weave, stiff, elaborate), damask (flat jaquard weave, elaborate designs, reversible), doublecloth (two fabrics interwoven), honeycomb, lamé (soft satin weave, metallic yarns added), leno (name of weaving machine, open patterned weave), matelessé (quilted-look, double weave), embossed fabrics (look like matelessé), tapestry (jaquard loom elaborate scenic, no luster).

Twill weaves
Long overshots in regular patterns create diagonal rows.

Bedford cord, denim, drill (plain cotton), gabardine, serge, surrah (soft, silky), whipcord.

Textured fabrics
Texture results from: textured yarns, pattern weaves, different amounts of shrinkage, large yarns, a loose weave, or surface fibers.

Crepe (twisted yarns make pebbly surface), bouclé (loopy bouclé yarns, knitted or woven, light to heavy), seersucker (alternate rows shrunk causes crinkle), chinchilla (curled nubs), crash (loose weave, irregular yarns), hopsacking (open basket weave, coarse yarns), monk's cloth (loose basket weave, heavy yarns), Ottoman (heavy rib), piqué (crisp, pattern weave, light to medium, cotton), pongee (wild silk yarns), shantung (slub yarns, lustrous), terry cloth (loopy surface, woven or knitted).

Stretchy
All fabrics stretch some, due to flexibility. Woven ones stretch on bias, knits stretch due to weave, others stretch due to fiber (spandex, rubber), or fiber resilience (crinkly wool).

Balbriggan (knit), bouclé (knit with loopy yarns), single knit (very stretchy), doubleknit (stretch one way), spandex fabrics.

Open Weave
Results from loose weaving, netting, twining, or finishes applied.

Burlap (jute), leno weaves (curtains), scrim (theater backdrops), cheesecloth (very light weight, soft), surrah (loose twill weave), net (knotted), needlepoint canvas, latch hook rug backing.

Non-fraying
Firmly woven, knitted or bonded edges will not come apart when cut. These fabrics also stretch less, have good dimensional stability.

Felt (non woven), doubleknits, fulled wool (felted), permanent press fabrics, bonded fabrics (two layers), laminated or surface decorated fabrics (suede cloth, flocked upholstery). Most synthetics are heat sealed for good stability.

above: Scissors by the author. *6″ long. The cut edges of felt do not fray and need not be turned to make a stuffed object. Machine stitching outlines the forms.*

below: My Opals, William's Pearls by Karen Reese. *7′ wide, 7′ high, 6″ deep. Tubular forms constructed of hand dyed satin, velvet, silk, polished cotton, and organza are stitched together and stuffed. The translucent organza allows colored stuffing to show through.*

Tools

SEWING TOOLS

Scissors — Buy good quality scissors and be careful not to cut wire or to drop them as tips break and blades misalign. Use two or three sizes including dressmaker shears, embroidery scissors, sewing scissors, or spring clippers for snipping threads.

Pins — Use good small sharp pins for fine fabrics, heavy longer pins for thicker ones, and hat pins for center pinning in quilting. Safety pins will not work out of fabric as you manipulate it. Colorful plastic heads make pins easier to locate. Use a magnet to collect them. To sew over straight pins by machine, place them at right angles to the stitch line. Hand wheel over them if you do not have a hinged sewing machine foot.

Sewing Machine — Shop carefully for a good reliable machine. It should stitch evenly, be easy to use, zigzag, and sew all weights of fabric. Fancy patterned stitches are not necessary. Always keep the machine manual close at hand to help solve sewing problems and to get the most out of your machine.

Measures — Get a good flexible tape measure (to measure around forms), a yard stick or metal ruler (for straight lines or calculating patterns), and perhaps a small calculator (to help make patterns, multiply dimensions, divide sections).

Needles — These come in all types: small eye sharps, long eye embroidery, curved upholstery, blunt tapestry, big yarn, wire thin beading, and assorted packets. Sewing machine needles also come in a range of sizes and points: sharp, general use, ball point (for knits), blade (to pierce leather), and combination double or triple needles.

Hoops and Frames — They help keep fabric flat for hand or machine embroidery, quilting, and other techniques.

Steam Iron — Buy a wide based iron that resists tipping over and is self cleaning. Press wrinkles from fabrics before cutting patterns or stuffing.

WORKSHOP TOOLS

Pliers — Small needle-nose pliers help pull a needle through tough material. Use larger pliers to bend and cut armature wires.

Hammer — A small tack hammer affixes fabric to

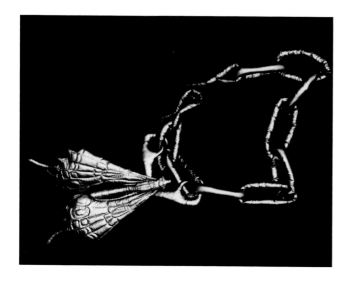

left: Charm Bracelet by Phyllis Varineau. 76″ wide, 4″ high, 3″ thick chain; 22″ wide, 14″ high, 2½″ thick charm. Tightly woven gold nylon parka fabric gives the metallic effect for this super-sized insect jewelry.

below left: Bride by Jeanne Boardman Knorr. 30″ wide, 5′ high, 6″ deep. Metallic and velvet fabrics draped over a metal armature symbolize royal personages inspired by visiting Versailles Gardens and Palace.

below right: Gargoyle by Pat Lehman. 15″ high. An assortment of rich decorative fabrics are appliqued, stitched, and stuffed into an abstract figure with a tiny papier-mâché face.

above: *Stegasaurus* by Kathryn Dyble Thompson. 17″ wide, 9″ high, 5″ thick. This dinosaur doll has a sturdy leather body, firmly stuffed, and embellished with toes and back plates of raku ceramic. Photographer, Jack Gajewski.

below: *Black Panther* by Rosalie Sherman. 27″ wide, 22″ high, 58″ long. "I wanted to make a scary, sexy, life-sized male, a nightmare creature." The black satin skin stretches tightly over a muslin layer which is stuffed with fiberfill. Aluminum tubing provides a full armature for the piece.

wooden backing. Use a larger hammer to assemble armatures.

Staple Gun — This tool aids in upholstery, framing, and making armatures. Staples come in different lengths and different strengths.

Cutters — Matt knives cut along a hard edge through heavy fabric. Paper cutters or rug cutters trim long narrow strips of fabric. Wire cutters or tin snips cut wire or sheet metal (wear gloves).

Saws — A coping saw cuts small wood, Masonite, matt board, or plastic foam. A saber saw cuts intricate designs in plywood, etc. A circular saw makes straight cuts in heavy materials. Handle power tools with extreme care.

OTHER TOOLS

Certain techniques require special tools: crochet hook, yarn shuttle, bodkin, loom, knitting needles, paint brush, drafting equipment, plumbing equipment, drills, nails, furniture accessories. You never can tell what tool will come in handy or how you can use one tool for another task.

Keep tools clean and sharp. Be sure to put them away, and do not use them for tasks that will damage them for their right use.

Other Equipment

You may need a step stool or step ladder (to reach or look down on large pieces), a large table or floor space (for cutting patterns, laying out designs), good lighting, space to work, a vent fan for fumes from painting and cleaning, and storage space for all those items collected and saved that might come in handy someday. Do not despair if you lack some of the listed equipment. Plenty of soft sculpture is made in the kitchen, dorm room, or on the move. Soft sculptors improvise because each new piece brings new problems.

above: Little Nell by the author. 6″ wide, 16″ tall, 12″ deep. One of the *Nine Cats* series, this cat combines both fiber and fabric. Strands of tightly twisted wool yarn were machine sewn into a long fringe which was then hand sewn onto the fabric body of the Persian cat.

Care of Soft Sculpture

Dust pieces often and gently to prevent a build-up of hard to remove airborn dirt. Spray-coat finished pieces with silicone (Scotchgard) to repel spills. To remove water soluble stains, rub with a sponge dipped in soap suds (no water) so the fabric does not get wet. Wet spots that dry slowly make a ring stain so use a hair dryer to speed drying. For extreme soil you may have to unstuff the piece depending upon how it is made, wash it, restuff, and then spray with silicone. Try various spot removers for greasy stains. Again, to prevent ring stains, avoid wetting the fabric. Consult cleaning manuals for specific information about types of stains and types of fabrics. Remove stains quickly before they set.

Do not display soft sculpture in bright sunlight or brightly reflected southern sun. Colors fade and fabrics rot. Soft sculpture begs to be touched but try to discourage people from touching since hand oils attract dirt. Avoid storing pieces in a hot attic or a damp basement. Cover heirloom pieces with a plastic box or frame made to size.

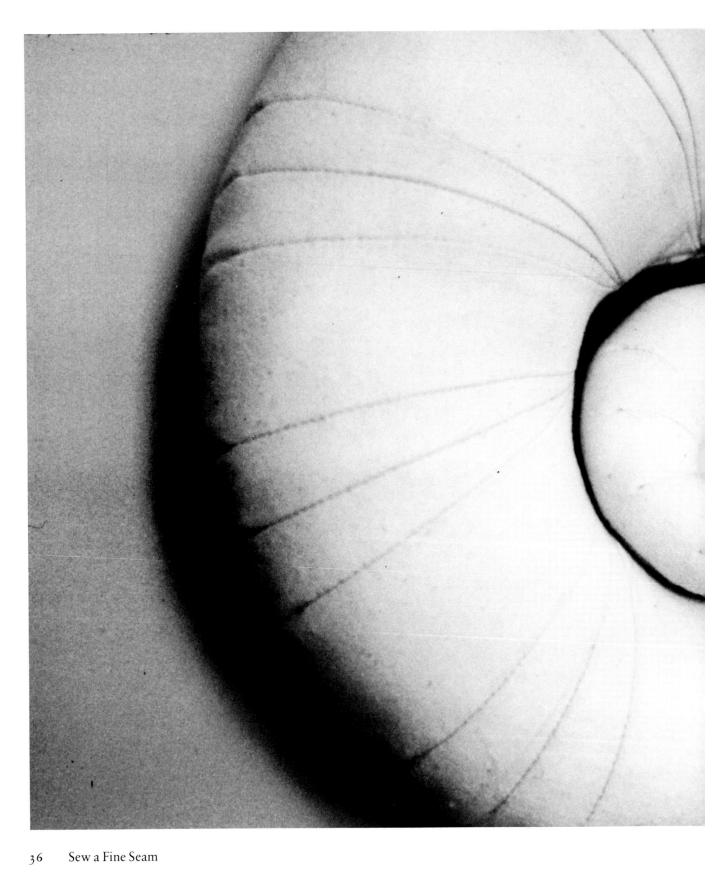

Chapter 4
Sew a Fine Seam

Seams must be well sewn before stuffing a soft sculpture as you will not be able to work on them from the reverse side again. Good seams have three main characteristics in common: (1) they are sewn with strong threads; (2) the stitches and type of seam hold firmly; and (3) the seam allowances are well trimmed, which avoids distortion.

Threads

Strong threads keep seams from popping open when pulled or tightly stuffed. Several kinds of thread are readily available for this purpose including: regular cotton, tough nylon, stretchy polyester, or core wrapped sewing thread. My favorite, core wrapped sewing thread, has a monofilament polyester core for strength. It is wrapped in mercerized cotton fibers, which give it flexibility, rich colors, and easy handling. Use the elastic polyester thread for seams that need to stretch. Embroidery threads for decorative use come in cotton or silk in many colors, sizes (diameters), and types.

Types of Seams

STRAIGHT STITCHING

Machine stitching usually makes a stronger seam than hand stitching since the top and bobbin threads clamp the fabric between them. Short stitches hold a seam tighter than long ones. To reinforce, overstitch with a second row of stitches at points of stress (corners or curves), or along an entire seam.

ZIGZAG STITCHING

Narrow or wide zigzag stitching helps prevent a seam from fraying or pulling. Zigzag stitching may pull apart since stitches run at right angles to the seam. To prevent this, sew a row of straight stitching on the seam line, then zigzag stitch next to it in the seam allowance. Some machines have a special overcast stitch that combines both steps.

left: Król I Królowa by Nettie Kobus. 40″ high. Artist's canvas, cut to shape and seamed intermittently, creates a stuffed shape strong enough to need no armature. Detail shows seams that shape fabric as well as provide a ribbed support.

above left: We Are What We Seam by Timmy Roman. 9″ wide, 9″ tall, 15″ long. Washable white felt was cut to shape with non-fraying edges exposed and hand stitched together — a do-it-yourself project.

above right: Group Picture-People by Ann Watson. 10″ wide, 14″ high, 3″ deep. Clothes for these portrait people were made from favorite clothing recut to fit tiny bodies and were seamed in clothing construction manner. Faces show various types of embroidery threads and yarns.

left: Cabbage Pillow, by Jean Gillies. Life-sized. Natural forms provide a wealth of design patterns for artists to enjoy, use and learn from. Hand quilted leaves in related green fabrics enfold a ball core.

Reinforcement

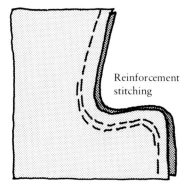

Reinforcement stitching

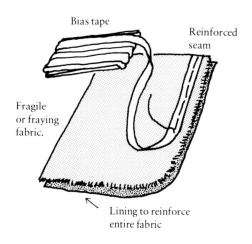

Bias tape

Reinforced seam

Fragile or fraying fabric.

Lining to reinforce entire fabric

above: Ruby by Ann Kingsbury. 12′ high. Leather provides a non-fraying firm but flexible material to model the lively body shape. The artist solves the problems of stitching tiny facial details by making a ceramic raku face for her mythical creature.

BACKING

For fabrics that may fray or pull out on the seams, such as burlap, satin weaves, or pile fabrics, you may need a separate fabric backing in addition to the reinforcement. Backing with bias tape or ribbon only may be sufficient. However, you may need to back the entire fabric with sheeting, lining, or interfacing (tailor's canvas, pellon).

OVERLAP SEAMS

These seams utilize the fabric strength for additional support. A simple overlap works best with non-supple materials (leather, mylar, or paper). To make this seam, place one edge overlapping the adjoining edge by ¼″ or more, then stitch a single, double, or zigzag row to hold it in place.

WELT SEAMS

Double overlap seams, similar to those on your jeans, are stronger than the fabric itself. To make them, place right sides of the fabric together, then stitch a straight seam on the seam line. Press or fold both seam allowances to the same side. Top stitch through all three layers (two seam allowances and one top fabric) for a strong flat seam. To eliminate raw edges on the reverse side, fold the seam allowance before stitching. This means you will stitch through five layers. If your machine cannot handle this, trim the under seam allowance shorter, then fold the top seam allowance to meet it, resulting in three layers to sew through. Vary the top stitching by using two rows of straight stitching or a row of zigzag stitching.

Overlap Seams

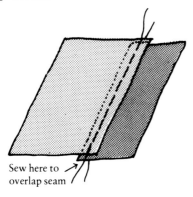

Sew here to overlap seam →

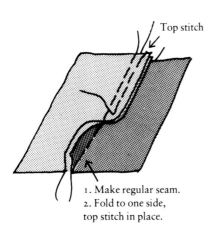

Top stitch

1. Make regular seam.
2. Fold to one side, top stitch in place.

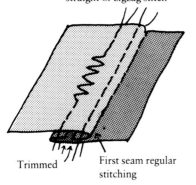

Top stitch (optional 2nd row) straight or zigzag stitch

Trimmed

First seam regular stitching

FRENCH SEAMS

This strong seam gives a finished look on the reverse side and prevents fraying. Sheer or decorative fabrics might require both. To do this, place fabric pieces back to back. Sew the seam midway between the seam line and the fabric edge on the face side of the fabric. Trim the seam allowance to less than ¼″. Turn the fabric and press the seam so it forms the edge. Stitch along the seam line on the back of the fabric sealing the trimmed seam inside. Welt and French seams may be too bulky for curves and corners.

STRETCHING SEAMS

Fabrics flex to varying degrees, allowing you to stretch a seam as needed. To stretch a seam as you sew, use a short stitch and pull with equal tension on both ends of the seam. Be careful not to pull on the sewing machine needle or it may break. Use stretchy threads for knit fabrics.

Zigzag stitching on the bias may stretch the seam without any help from you. To prevent this, stretch the fabric in a hoop to stitch or sew over backing paper which can be torn off at needle perforations.

SHORTENING SEAMS

"Ease" means to shorten a seam without causing wrinkles. To ease, make a row of long stitches (through one or both layers as needed). Pull the looser thread, spacing the fullness along the seam to the required length. This allows a longer seam to fit a shorter one. The longer side will be fuller and curve toward the shorter one.

If none of these techniques work, consider stapling, riveting, punching and lacing, or gluing fabrics in place.

Trimming

Incorrectly trimmed seam allowances produce ugly wrinkles or add strange lumps to soft sculpture. Seam allowance widths (varying from ¼″ to ¾″) are determined by the weave of the fabric. Loose weaves that might fray need wider seam allowances to keep seams from pulling out. Most seam allowances will not need trimming. Those that constrict a turned seam, especially at curves or corners, need careful trimming.

CURVES

Stitch curves with short stitches so seams will not pull apart. Make small clipped slashes almost to the seam line. This allows the seam allowance to stretch around the

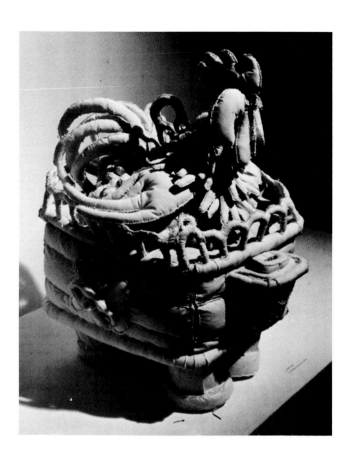

left: Rooster Music Box by Randall Schade. 18″ high. A series of stuffed flat shapes, hand sewn with raw edges, assembles into a sculptured rooster machine of considerable charm. Lift a flap on the side to wind the music box inside. Made from off white, unbleached muslin fabric.

French Seam

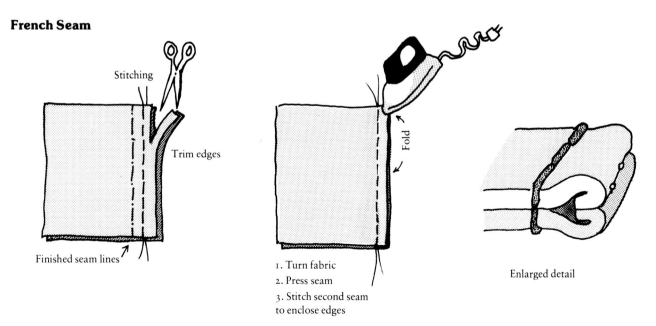

Stitching

Trim edges

Finished seam lines

Fold

1. Turn fabric
2. Press seam
3. Stitch second seam to enclose edges

Enlarged detail

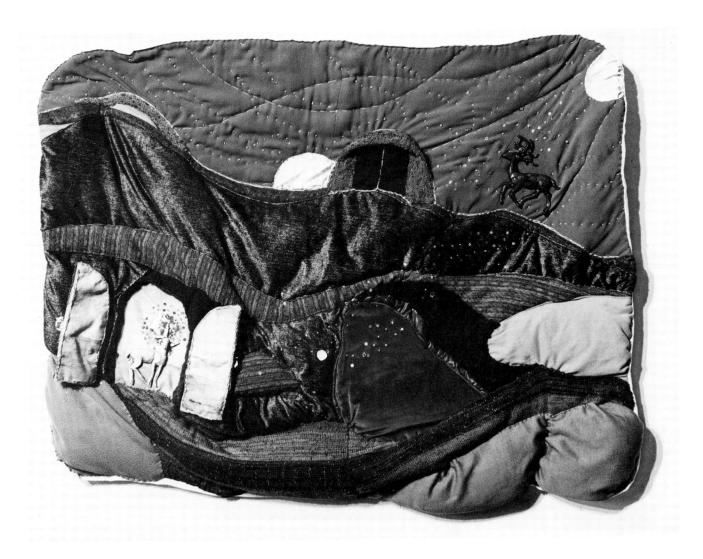

The Doors of Perception by Elsbeth Ramos. 3½′ by 3′. Velvets and other fabrics selected for color and texture and appliquéd to the backing, then trapunto stuffed. Deer figures were molded of "oven clay," baked, then applied to the hanging.

Trimming Outside Curves

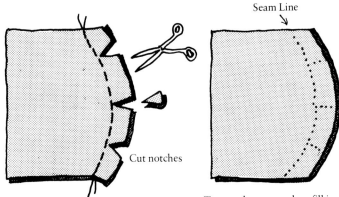

Cut notches

Seam Line

Turn and press notches, fill in to make a smooth surface.

Ease

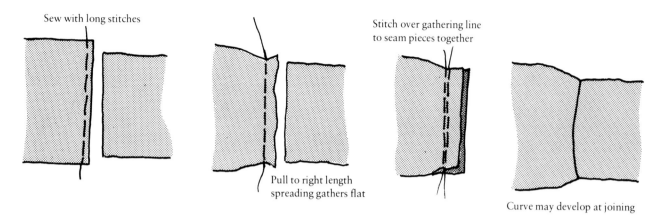

Sew with long stitches

Pull to right length spreading gathers flat

Stitch over gathering line to seam pieces together

Curve may develop at joining

Trimming Inside Curves

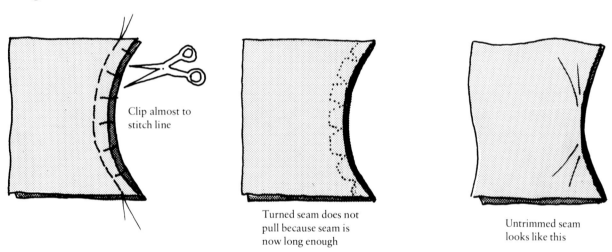

Clip almost to stitch line

Turned seam does not pull because seam is now long enough

Untrimmed seam looks like this

Trimming Corners

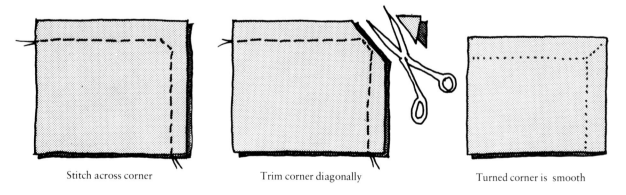

Stitch across corner

Trim corner diagonally

Turned corner is smooth

Trimming Sharp Corners

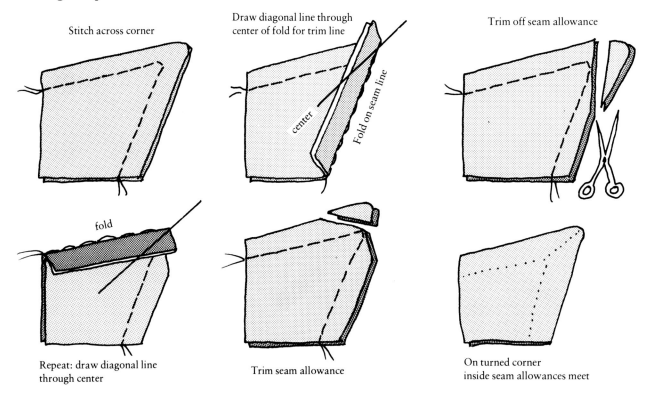

Stitch across corner

Draw diagonal line through center of fold for trim line

center

Fold on seam line

Trim off seam allowance

fold

Repeat: draw diagonal line through center

Trim seam allowance

On turned corner inside seam allowances meet

Adding Fabric: Gussets

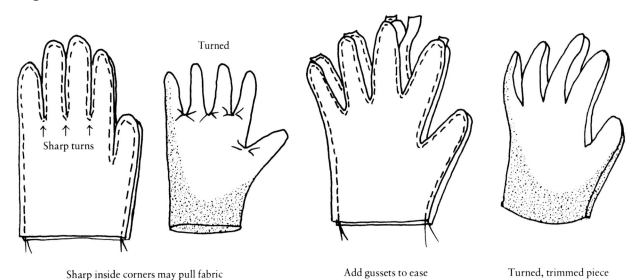

Sharp turns

Turned

Sharp inside corners may pull fabric when piece is turned.

Add gussets to ease pull at sharp turns.

Turned, trimmed piece is smoother.

above left: White Phalaenopsis by Pat Maloney. 3' across. This softly colored giant orchid conceals its properly stitched and trimmed inside seams. Improperly trimmed seams show on the exterior by wrinkles and pulled seams.

above right: Pig In A Poke by Kit Flannery. 19" diameter. Pink suede fabric is sewed and glued to a metal hoop and stuffed for a soft art pig portrait. Owner Peggy Thomas.

curve. If your fabric does not fray trim the seam allowance very close to the stitch line around the curve.

For outside curves with so much seam allowance that it might bunch into lumps, cut notches at close intervals almost to the seam line.

CORNERS

For a neat, strong corner, stitch with regular or small stitches almost to the corner, turn the fabric 45 degrees, stitch two stitches, turn 45 degrees to complete a square corner, and continue the seam. Clip the seam allowance across the corner close to the two stitches.

To trim a sharper corner, fold the seam allowance over the corner at the seam line (as it will eventually be folded when the piece is turned). Draw a diagonal line on the seam allowance from the center to the corner to see how much you need to trim away. Do the same with the other seam allowance. If the corner seam pulls apart when turned, reinforce the stitches and trim away additional seam allowance or sew the corner less sharply.

OTHER CORNERS

Sometimes a corner must be very sharp indeed as in the case of a fabric cut for glove fingers. To diminish strain on a corner like this, add a gusset, insert a piece of fabric, or make a seam at this point. The added seam allows for more shaping of pattern pieces. More information on cutting pattern pieces follows in Chapter 6.

Sew a Fine Seam   45

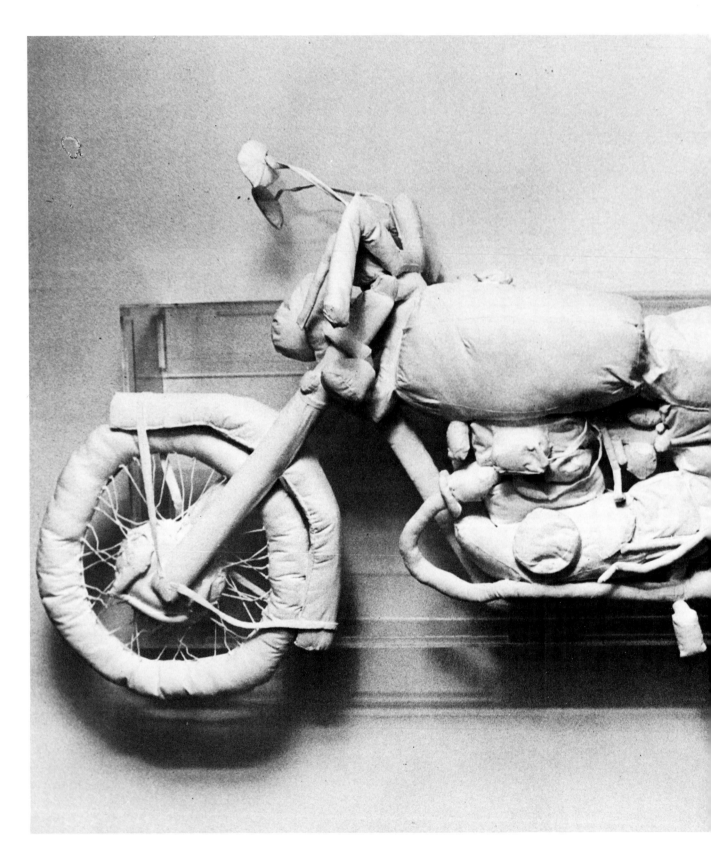

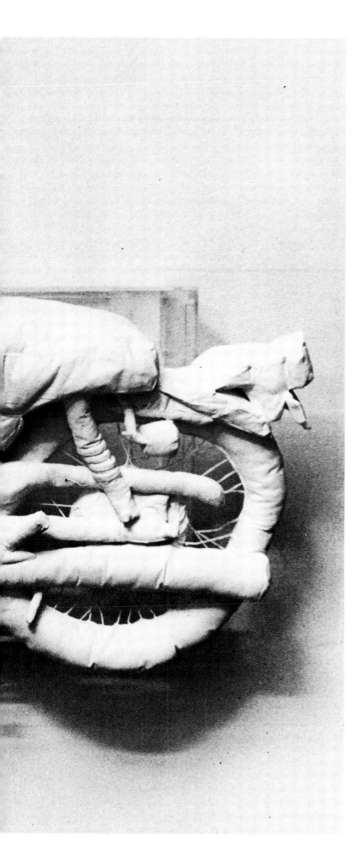

Chapter 5
Stuffing Materials

Insides are as important as outsides in shaping soft sculpture. Lumpy stuffings mean lumpy surfaces. It takes the right stuffing pushed properly in place to get the best effect. This chapter describes the characteristics of a wide assortment of stuffings and fillers, gives methods for stuffing, and lists handy tools for poking them into place.

Stuffings vary in character from heavy to light, shifting to firm, resilient to solid, or long lasting to ephemeral. Each soft sculpture may require a different kind of filler or even need two or three different kinds of stuffings in one piece to make it look right. The stuffing chart will help you make correct choices.

Polyester ranks as the most popular stuffing by far because of its many fine qualities. A look at the labels on toys, pillows, and furniture reveals that almost anything can stuff an object — for example, crushed shells, newspapers, chopped plants, and "unidentified materials."

Among traditional stuffings, antique china-headed dolls had soft bodies with sawdust inside, and Teddy bears were firmly packed with shaved wood called excelsior. Today, beds can be filled with water, and balloons with hot air. Consider any possibility for stuffing.

Tools for Stuffing

Most shapes stuff well by hand, but small shapes like fingers require a long narrow tool to push filler all the way to the end. Several possible objects for this purpose include: scissors, a large knitting needle, a pencil (with no lead point), a sharpened dowel stick, or artist's paint brush handle (use a pencil sharpener for a good point). Be careful not to poke through the covering, especially with the scissors.

To stuff with a tool, place or wrap a small wad of fiberfill on the end. Insert the wad tipped tool into the opening and push the wad into place. To avoid lumps, fill the shape little by little. To smooth a lumpy piece, roll it

left: Honda 350 by Susan Anson. 72″ long, 36″ high, 12″ deep. Soft art has wide appeal. *Honda* was commissioned by Cycle World Magazine for an advertisement, which also appeared in the 1976 *Communications Arts Annual*. Photographer, David Cooley.

STUFFING CHART

Stuffing	Information	Character
Polyester Fiber Petroleum based synthetic spun into monofilament fibers then chopped into staple fibers	Many good qualities: handles easily, springs back from crushing (resilient), weighs little, is non-absorbent (so it washes well, dries quickly), is readily available in stores everywhere at reasonable cost. Comes in bags of one pound or more.	little shifting, light weight, washable in thin layers.
Polyester batts Dacron trade name	Comes in quilt sized layer of fibers about ½″ thick. Pulls apart easily.	little shifting, light weight, washable.
Polyester bonded batts	Quilt sized layer of fibers about ½″ thick. Fibers are bonded together to prevent shifting, requires less quilting, cut with scissors to shape.	non-shifting, light weight, washable.
Polyester Upholstery batts	Rolls 2″ thick sandwiched and quilted between layers of cheesecloth. To shape, cut with scissors.	non-shifting, lightweight, washable (as in loose quilting.)
Rubberized Hair Horse hair sprayed with rubberized coating.	Sheets 1-3″ thick, used for upholstery. Very resilient and airy. Cut with heavy scissors.	non-shifting, light weight.
Cotton Fibers Part of seed pod of cotton plant.	Comes in top quality bleached white or in natural with a few seeds still imbedded. Not very resilient, absorbs moisture, handles easily. Comes in batts, bags, boxes, or balls.	little shifting, washable in thin sheets, fairly light weight.
Wool Fibers Hair from many animals, sheep, camels, goats, llamas, etc.	Springy fibers remain lofty to hold body heat. Easy to handle. Felts naturally. Attracts moths.	little shifting, washable with care in thin layers, medium weight.
Feathers Comes from birds, mainly chickens and geese.	Favorite for pillows, comforters, jackets. Highly resilient when new. Warm. Soft under feathers called *down* are softest. For more firmness stiffer, larger feathers are mixed in or used entirely.	very shifting, light weight, wash with extreme care.
Molded Foam Rubber Natural rubber foamed full of tiny air bubbles.	Comes in sheets and slabs, and in varying degrees of density for softness. Larger holes sometimes molded into the slab give added softness, less weight. Cut with scissors, electric knife, hot wire, or saw.	non-shifting, medium to heavy weight, deteriorates with wear.
Molded Foam Polyurethane Petroleum based plastic.	Comes in many sizes and shapes: thin sheets, 4 to 6″ slabs, pillow, or cushion forms. Cut with scissors, bread knife, hack saw, etc. Sew thin sheets with sewing machine. Resists deterioration better than foam rubber but is not as resilient.	non-shifting, light weight.
Shredded Foam Polyurethane or foam rubber.	Inexpensive, lumpy, light weight, messy to handle, very resilient. (Use as inner core with smoother stuffing or liner outside.)	shifting, light weight.
Kapok fibers From seed of kapok tree.	Inexpensive, non-absorbent (formerly popular), non-resilient.	shifting, light weight.

above: Three Dolls by Rae Holzman. 16″ wide, 20″ high, 8″ deep. "I make people to show ourselves as we are." These "fun or reality" portraits, commissioned for *Rags*, are hand and machine sewn of panty hose knit fabric, assorted yarns and fabrics, and stuffed with polyester fiberfill. Photographer, Tom Liden.

Plant material Straw, leaves, grass, vines, weeds.	Freely available, non-resilient, may crumble. Be sure this is clean, dry material.	may shift (depends upon shape and size of stuffing), light to medium weight.
Herbs and dried flowers	Aromatic, non-resilient, crumbles with wear.	shifting, light weight.
Seeds Dried peas, beans, popcorn, lentils, rice, pepper corns, acorns, walnuts, pine cones, etc.	Keep seeds dry. Use only tightly woven fabric skin. Non-resilient.	very shifting, medium to light weight.
Other food stuffs Spaghetti, macaroni, noodles, salt	Be sure to keep clean and dry. Non-resilient.	very shifting, very heavy.
Sand, gravel, clay pellets (Kitty Litter)	Use tightly woven, strong covering. Non-resilient.	very shifting, very heavy.
Expanded vermiculite	Used for insulation or potting plants. Non-resilient.	very shifting, light weight.
Rags, old clothes, stockings	Use whole or tear into sections. May have a little resilience depending upon fiber content.	little shift, medium weight.
Foam pellets Polystyrene	Use for bean bag chairs. Have no resiliency but lots of shift. Attracts static electricity and sticks to everything when loose.	very light weight, shifting.
Saw dust or chips	Firm, non-resilient.	shifting unless solidly packed, medium to heavy.

above left: Self-Portrait, Claudia Hall. 12″ square, 6″ deep, *15 Boxes* series. A pink cloud of insulation material stuffing floats behind clear vinyl. Polyester fiberfill stuffing is pushed into quilted channels, trapunto style. A wooden box provides an armature, a mirror behind the eyes of the photograph, appliquéd to the fabric, reflects your own eyes back.

above right: Forgotten Road by Elsbeth Ramos. 8′ by 10′. Softly stuffed wall hangings of mythical creatures that puff and wrinkle like a comforter give the effect of a bedtime story, a flight into a fantasy land. Photographer, Ron James. Courtesy, Vorpel Gallery.

between your hands. Sometimes you can push one long wad of batting into the entire shape in one motion.

To adjust stuffing already inside, insert a long sturdy sharp pointed needle through the covering, then shift the stuffing into place. To stuff narrow, quilted channels, sew filler in place from the back side using a blunt tapestry needle threaded with yarn.

Methods of Stuffing

HEAVY SHIFTING STUFFINGS

Heavy fillers can weight the bottom of soft sculpture or give pieces a solid weighted look. Heavy granular fillers, which include sand, kitty litter, and most of the seeds listed, pour easily into sewn shapes. These heavy fillers need sturdy coverings and strong seams to prevent leaks. Caution: they may distort stretchy fabrics.

To allay these problems, use a firm fabric (non-stretchy) and cut the shape carefully. Use a funnel or heavy paper rolled into a funnel shape to guide grains into the covering. Support the covering well during filling so it will not tip over. To avoid spills, stitch the opening closed immediately. For added protection against leaks, shifting, or broken seams, and to provide firmer support, use an inner lining bag sewn to shape.

above left: Vegimal by Beverly Red. 4″ long. The white velour egg shell zips open, and out pops the stuffing — a fried egg that unfolds because of the resilient fiberfill stuffing inside.

above right: Vegimal by Beverly Red. 8″ long. This soft corduroy velour fish has a hollow lining inside so he can swallow a smaller stuffed fish.

left: Nine Bags by the author. Each bag measures 19″ × 20″. Assorted stuffings include: polyester, foamed plastic pellets, shredded foam rubber, wadded tissue paper, raw sheep's wool, feathers, pine cones, gravel, and fur lining. Numbers are stippled on with acrylic paint. Notice how the stuffings affect the shape.

below: Bean Bag Baby by Brooke Greeson-Wilson. 3″ by 3½″. The special character of bean bags has been popular for generations. The shifting lumpy filler weights the base of the baby shown, allowing her to assume various poses. Her head and hands are ceramic; her dress is seersucker, a fabric woven with alternating rows that shrink.

Stuffing Materials   51

right: Pug Dog by the author. 11″ wide, 18″ long, 15″ high. A small wooden stool is used as an armature in this stuffed dog. Off white upholstery velvet simulate the pug's flat fur. Black velvet button eyes and nose nestle in the expressive wrinkles sewn into the dog's face.

center: Pug Dog. Materials assembled to model the stuffing for the dog include: a bonded batt of polyester fiberfill, staplegun and staples for fixing the stuffing to the wooden stool, a ball of string not shown, and old sheeting. Any materials can be added for bulk under the batting.

bottom: Pug Dog. Sharp corners were sawed off the wooden stool before beginning to wrap the legs. String binds the large sections of bonded batting in place while staples secure the underside.

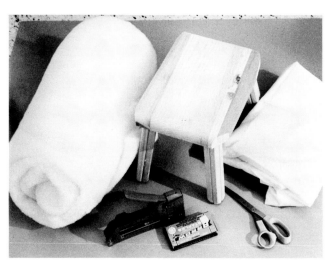

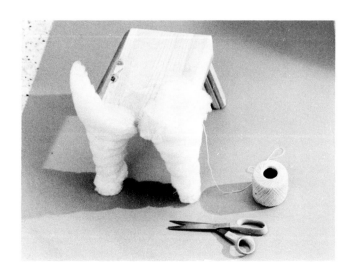

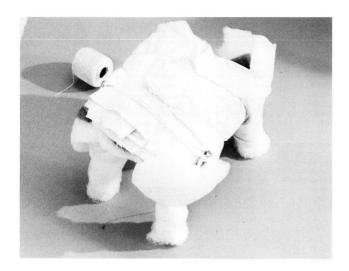

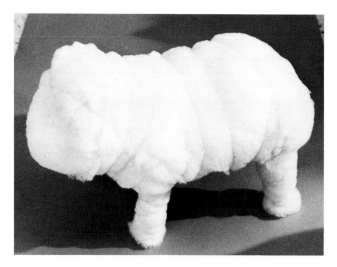

above left: Pug Dog. Old sheeting provides additional bulk for stuffing but does not compress softly. Stuffing is now too thick to use staples to hold it in place.

above right: Pug Dog. The base stuffing is now completed and ready for a lining layer of muslin if a stretchy skin will be used. The velvet upholstery used held firmly enough so an underlayer was not needed. Additional stuffing was eventually added under the skin fabric to complete the modeled shape.

LIGHT WEIGHT SHIFTING STUFFING

Use light weight granular stuffings for coverings made of delicate fabrics, for large volume pieces, or for a shifting effect without a weight. These fillers include: feathers, foam pellets, light sawdust, and shredded foam. They pour like heavier granules but need a larger funnel to avoid clogging. Because feathers float, pellets cling, and foam sticks to things, it is best to contain them well. Pin or sew the bag of filler to the opening in the covering, then shake the contents from bag to sculpture. In addition feathers or sawdust may require a firmly woven inner lining to prevent sifting or poking through.

NON-SHIFTING STUFFINGS

Materials such as polyester fiber, cotton, wool, rags, cleaner's bags, or excelsior stay in place better than granular stuffing; however, they do not pour into nooks and crannies. All shapes, even those as simple as pillows, require careful stuffing. A large wad will not fill corners and will lump in the middle, so for better results first fill the corners with smaller bits of stuffing. Use long wads along sides. Continue to fill the piece bit by bit to build the shape to the necessary fullness and firmness.

To stuff narrow shapes, such as fingers, begin to stuff them before you turn the whole piece. Turn all the fingers and stuff. Turn the hand and stuff. Turn the arm and stuff. Stuff feet, noses, heads and other protuberances in the same manner. Do not stuff beyond this before turning the rest of the piece as you may not be able to get the stuffed sections through the turning opening.

Necks on stuffed figures may flop. Use a tightly rolled wad of stuffing or something stiffer (a roll of cardboard or a small plastic bottle) for an armature. (See Chapter 7 on armatures.)

Stuffing Materials   53

above left: Superchair by Alice Leeds. Chairs, rarely applauded, get special attention from this artist. This red satin chair is softly stuffed over an armature and fitted with wings. Photographer, Joseph Yarzzo.

above right: Six Ladies by Elizabeth Gurrier. 24″ diameter. Finely done machine and hand sewn quilting on this white muslin floor pillow resembles the intricate quilting done by forebears in earlier centuries in America and Europe. Courtesy, Detroit Gallery of Contemporary Crafts. Photographer, Alpine Photographic.

left: A Month of Rainbows by Alice Leeds. 12″ wide, 8″ deep, 12″ high. Silver lamé stuffed gloves assist in opening the silver lamé box filled with thirty-one (for each day of the month) quilted rainbow pieces. The brightly hued satin rainbow days are embellished with machine embroidery over appliqué. Viewers are invited to participate. Photographer, Joseph Yarzzo.

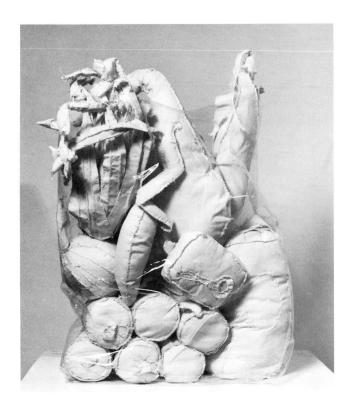

above: DDT by Randall Schade. 15" wide, 9" deep, 18" high. The clear plastic grocery bag allows an x-ray view of the contents. White muslin groceries are handsewn unturned shapes softly stuffed.

above: Summer 78 by Rosalie Shirley. 23" wide, 17" high, 17" deep. The brown paper box bursts open with a profusion of textures and colors to express the painful but exhilarating growth experience of a four week seminar with Joseph Grau-Garriga, Spanish textile artist. The artist took six months to refine the idea and collect materials, and one five-day burst to assemble it into a personal expression. Photographer, Ken Heywood.

SECTIONAL STUFFING

Muscles, knee caps, noses, or other full forms may need help to keep their stuffing in place, especially if the piece is softly stuffed. If the wad shifts, sew the stuffing wad to the inside seam allowance to conceal the stitches or sew a lining behind the wad to compartment it. Plan to make softly stuffed pieces in compartments so the filler will not sag out of place.

In quilting, the face fabric, stuffing and back fabric form a sandwich held together with a pattern of stitches. Close stitching on bonded batting keeps the filling from shifting. In trapunto, a form of quilting, added filler can be used to increase dimension in some areas. Stuffing is pushed into place through slits cut in the backing, which are then stitched shut.

COMBINATION STUFFINGS

Stretchy, sheer, or coarsely woven fabrics may fail to hold their shapes. For a firmer foundation, sew muslin under-shapes and stuff firmly or model the stuffing into shape by wrapping it with string, tape, or fabric. For the firmest foundation, cut shapes from bonded batts or from molded foams.

You may need to combine stuffings to get the best qualities of both or solve special problems. Some sofa cushions have a foam rubber core wrapped in a soft polyester batting; others have a cloud of downy feathers contained by a "box" of foam rubber to keep the shape.

Soft sculpture pieces sometimes need two different kinds of stuffing, one to weight the bottom of a piece for stability, another light one to fill the top.

OTHER STUFFING IDEAS

Soft sculptures, like full tummies, are essentially rounded shapes. It takes effort and a firm stuffing such as foam slabs to make a flat sided stuffed piece. One way to model soft shapes is by sewing dimples and noses in place by needle and thread from an opposite side. Stocking figures show this technique quite clearly. (See Chapter 9 for specific detail.)

Since stuffings are so important in most sculpture, it is not surprising that innovative stitchers conceived the idea of exposing the stuffing. Clear plastic (mylar) or transparent fabrics sewn by hand or machine, stapled, riveted, or laced allows them to do this. Choose interesting textures to fill these pieces: sand, sea shells, excelsior, cut paper, natural cotton, unspun wool, or popped corn.

It helps to think about stuffing problems in advance so you can plan for them. Each different piece presents a unique set of requirements.

Stuffing Materials 55

Chapter 6
Pattern Making

Fabric soft sculptures consist of variously shaped pieces of cloth sewn together and stuffed. Flat figures take no more fabric than is needed to trace around, but full round figures require more complicated pattern pieces and more fabric.

This chapter shows how to shape fabrics into forms, to estimate amounts of fabric required, and to make a pattern for a three-dimensional form from a flat drawing.

Soft sculptors use three main methods to make their own patterns. They alter existing patterns to their needs. They cut and fit the fabric pieces by trial and error. They develop a pattern from a preliminary drawing by measuring and computing. Most use a combination of the three. All three methods share similar basics.

Patterns

A pattern provides a guide for cutting fabrics into shape. Patterns also allow space for recording necessary markings such as: seam allowances, number of pieces to cut, darts or gathers, where pieces join, and notations for decoration. Be sure to follow the seam allowances and other markings accurately to achieve the desired results.

Paper and cloth make the best patterns. Both are flexible, light weight, and cost little. They can be marked on, pinned through, and folded for storage. Any kind of paper will do: tissue paper, tracing paper, newspaper, grocery bags, and wrapping paper. For stronger patterns use a firm fabric like sheeting, non-woven interfacing, or plastic film. Templates, stiff patterns made from cardboard, stiff plastic, or similar materials wear longer and are easy to trace around. However, you cannot pin through templates.

Alterations

Modifying a simple square pattern presents few problems since you can add or subtract the necessary amount from

left: Trapeze Artists by Cynthia Nixon-Hudson. Each 9″ tall. Part of a troupe, these painted muslin figures appear to hang weightlessly on monofilament line. Notice that cutting the head, body and arms in one unit solves many construction problems. Photographer, Jeanne Steven-Sollman.

above left: Self-Portrait by Lynn DiNino. 5′ 8″ tall, 18″ wide, 10″ thick. "It's creepy to have a life-sized stuffed figure of yourself sitting in your living room, but it makes a great burglar deterrent!"

above right: Emma by Cindy Hickok. Life-sized. Soft sculpture provides an ideal technique for expressing the soft wrinkled visages of older people. Everybody likes to have a grandmother in a rocking chair around the house.

Alterations

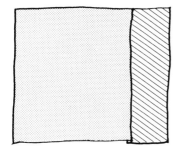

Add onto edge of simple patterns.

one side. More complex patterns require changes made at a mid point to maintain the pattern outline. The four basic methods used to alter patterns are (1) tuck, (2) cut and insert, (3) dart, (4) slash and insert. For example:

(1) To shorten a duck pattern fold a tuck across the pattern so the edges align. Pin in place, then cut or trace around the pattern. If tuck edges fail to line up exactly, smooth the outline as you cut or trace.

(2) To lengthen, cut across the pattern and insert a section of paper (or fabric). Pin, tape, or glue the insert in place. To keep the original pattern intact, trace around one half, move the pattern the required amount, then trace around the rest of the outline. Do this on paper for a new pattern or directly on the fabric.

(3) To widen in one area, make a deep slash in the pattern, then insert paper. Pin, tape, or glue in place and smooth pattern outlines as you trace or trim around it.

(4) To reduce size in one section, fold a long dart then pin it in place. Make sure the pattern lays flat.

Fold a tuck in pattern to shorten.

Insert a section to lengthen

Slash pattern and insert a section to increase in one area.

Fold a dart to shorten in one area.

Shaping

Flat patterns sewn into forms may wrinkle at the seams if stuffed too fully. They need additional contouring to make a full round form. To create fullness within the pattern use darts, gathers, or gussets.

(1) Darts (triangular tucks) decrease the outline length and create fullness. (See diagram.) Mark darts with dotted lines. Trim away excess fabric in the dart if needed.

(2) For gathers, sew long stitches on the seam line, then pull the thread to gather the seam shorter. If no wrinkles result, this is called "easing." This allows a longer seam to fit a shorter one. (Sleeve elbows are often eased on one side to create elbow room.) Easing works best on soft weaves, stretchy fabrics, or bias cuts since gathering wrinkles are less apt to show.

(3) A small insert, called a gusset, gives added fullness and strength at points of stress. Cut a slash or "U" in the outline. Insert a fan-shaped piece.

SEAMS

Additional seams within a pattern give more chance for shaping. For example, slash across the duck pattern (see diagram) then add a long half circle to each side of the slash. Do not forget to include seam allowances. When curves are sewn together, the bird body will puff up like a football. Additional seams make an ideal place to add other pieces, like wings. To do this, complete the added piece first. To stitch it in place, pin the wing onto the face side of one body half, with raw edges over the seam. Pin the other body half in place face to face. Stitch seam closed. This leaves no raw edge exposed.

Seams become part of the design, so place them carefully and logically. For example, make a seam down the center of a face to allow for a protruding nose or insert a fan-shaped nose with seam lines cut along natural crease lines.

Measuring Basic Patterns

Full round soft sculpture figures need more complex pattern pieces than flat ones to achieve their shapes. To determine what shape to cut patterns and how much fabric to buy, you need to measure the surface area. With existing pieces this is easy to do with a tape measure. For

Darts

Stuffed duck wrinkles because outline is too long.

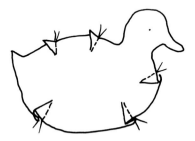

Make darts to decrease outline length and add fullness.

Smoother stuffed result.

Ease

Gather seams slightly to shorten (see "ease" Chapter 4)

above: Waitress by Lynn DiNino. Life-sized. Synthetic suede knit fabric is carefully cut to pattern, machine sewn, then turned and stuffed. Eyelids and lips are added sections. The hamburger also has its portrait done in fabrics and fiberfill.

example, to cover a pillow or chair, measure the length and width of all the pieces needed, then fit these pieces on a diagram or the fabric you plan to use.

But how can you measure something that only exists in your head? Fortunately, mathematicians have worked out easy ways to measure and compute surface areas of geometric forms. We can use these same techniques to measure and make accurate patterns for soft sculpture.

Most soft sculpture consists of variations of four basic geometric shapes: the cube, sphere (ball), cone, and cylinder (tube). Check this by examining various examples in this book.

Tools you need to make patterns include: scratch paper, pencil, ruler or tape measure, compass, and pocket calculator if you have one.

CUBE

Draw a square the size you want the finished cube to measure. Measure one side of the square, then add seam allowances. For example, to make a four inch cube, add two ½″ seam allowances to equal 5 inches. A cube has six

Gussets

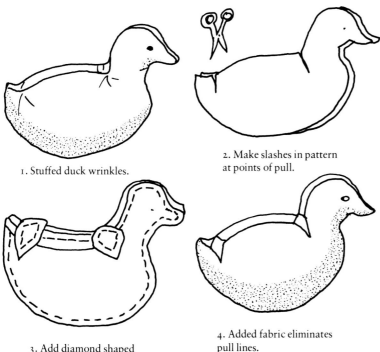

1. Stuffed duck wrinkles.

2. Make slashes in pattern at points of pull.

3. Add diamond shaped gussets.

4. Added fabric eliminates pull lines.

Add Fullness by Shaping

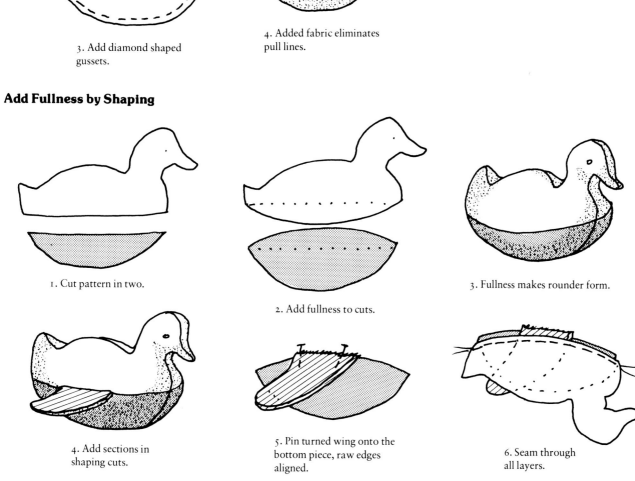

1. Cut pattern in two.

2. Add fullness to cuts.

3. Fullness makes rounder form.

4. Add sections in shaping cuts.

5. Pin turned wing onto the bottom piece, raw edges aligned.

6. Seam through all layers.

Most soft sculptures are made up of simple geometric forms (cube, tube, ball, cone) altered to need. To estimate fabric needs, reduce figures to geometric forms to compute fabric area for parts.

sides, so make six pieces each 5″ square. For this you need one piece of fabric 5″ wide by 30″ long, or one piece of fabric 10″ wide by 15″ long. Cut the piece into six squares.

Rule: Any cube will take six times as much fabric as the area of one side (plus seam allowances). For a double box lined on the inside, you would need twelve times as much.

SPHERE OR BALL

For a one-piece ball, draw a circle the size of the ball you want. Measure across the widest part of the circle to find the diameter. Multiply the diameter by 3.14 or pi on your calculator. (Pi is the mathematical formula for measuring circles. It means that circles measure just over three times as much around as wide.) For example, multiply a 4″ ball times 3.14 to get 12.56″. Add ½″ seam allowance all around to make a 13½″ circle pattern for the ball. (Numbers are rounded off to conform to rulers and tapes.) To complete the ball, sew long stitches ½″ in from the edge all the way around. Pull the thread tightly to gather into a ball. For this type of ball you need a piece of fabric 13½″ square.

Rule: A gathered ball will take over 9 times as much material as the area of the ball drawing, with some waste.

CONE

To make a cone, draw a triangle with 4″ sides. Double the 4″ to find the diameter of the circle needed,, then add seam allowances, for example 4″ + 4″ + ½″ + ½″ = 9″ circle. Use half of the 9″ circle for a cone pattern. Add a ½″ seam allowance to the straight side. This requires a piece of fabric 5″ by 9″. To sew the cone, fold the circle in half, then stitch along the straight edges. For a cone base you need a 5″ circle of fabric, including a seam allowance.

Rule: A cone takes about three times as much fabric as the area of its drawing, not including the base or waste. Note: Cutting several pieces together using efficient pattern placement diminishes fabric waste.

CYLINDER OR TUBE

Draw a 4″ wide square or rectangle to indicate the tube width. It can measure any length. Measure across the tube drawing for the diameter. Multiply 4″ times 3.14 to find the circumference or measurement around the tube. 4″ × 3.14 = 12.56″ + seam allowances (rounded off) = 13.5″. You will need a piece of fabric 13½″ wide by the length you choose. To sew the tube, fold the fabric in half lengthwise, then sew the seam opposite the fold closed.

Rule: A cylinder takes fabric that is about three and one-fourth times as wide as the diameter, by whatever length is needed, with no waste.

Cube

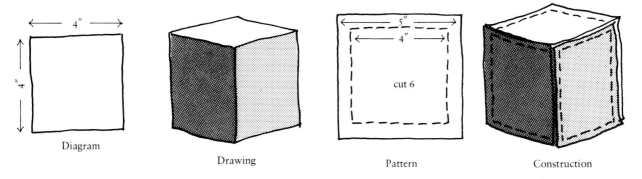

Diagram

Drawing

cut 6

Pattern

Construction

A cube takes six times as much fabric as the area of one side (plus seam allowances).

Ball

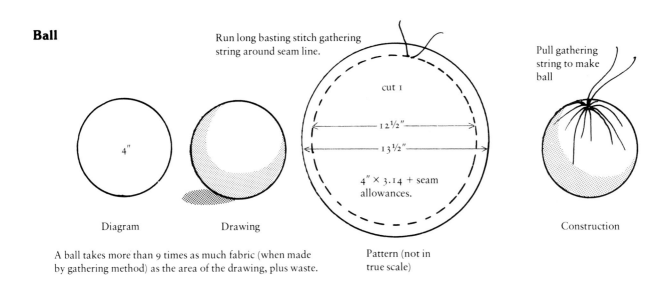

Run long basting stitch gathering string around seam line.

cut 1

12½″

13½″

4″ × 3.14 + seam allowances.

Pull gathering string to make ball

Diagram

4″

Drawing

Pattern (not in true scale)

Construction

A ball takes more than 9 times as much fabric (when made by gathering method) as the area of the drawing, plus waste.

Cone

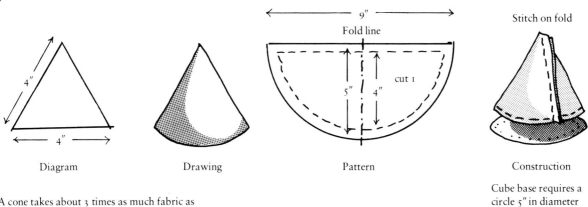

Diagram

4″ 4″

Drawing

9″

Fold line

cut 1

5″ 4″

Pattern

Stitch on fold

Construction

A cone takes about 3 times as much fabric as the area of the diagram (minus the base).

Cube base requires a circle 5″ in diameter (4″ plus seam allowance)

Tube

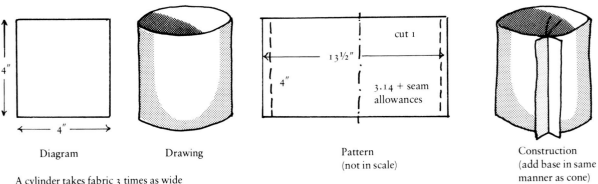

Diagram   Drawing   Pattern
                                                (not in scale)

Construction
(add base in same
manner as cone)

A cylinder takes fabric 3 times as wide
as the diagram plus seam allowances by whatever
length, with no waste.

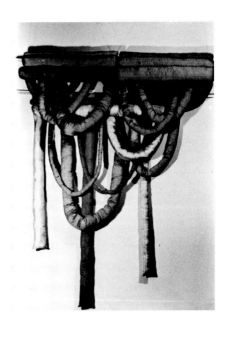

above left: Orange, Fuchsia, Yellow by Madge
Huntington. 48″ wide, 54″ high, 6″ deep. Various sizes and lengths of tubes, constructed of
opulent Thai silk and stuffed with fiberfill,
create a vivid abstract wall hanging.

above right: In The Beginning by Kathryn
McCardle Lipke. 24″ wide, 36″ long, 14″ thick.
Simple geometric shapes, the ball and tube,
create a sophisticated abstract soft sculpture.
Sheer natural linen fabric accepts the dye
screen printed design well and fills attractively
with soft stuffing.

above: *Vegetable Platter* by Linda Jackier. 32″ wide, 48″ high, 2″ thick. Batik resist dyeing, highlighted by dye painting on 100% China silk, then stuffed and outline quilted, glows with color. Photographer, the artist.

right: Three Cats from *Nine Cats* by Carolyn Hall. Each cat 6′ wide, 12′ long, 15′ high. Three of the nine cats show variations on the basic form. The surface treatment catches the character of various well-remembered cats by embroidery, tie dye, crochet and varied colors.

above: Madame Butterfly by Phyllis Varineau. 34″ wide, 24″ high. Appliqué, trapunto quilting, and stuffing comprise this comical character. Photographer, the artist.

right: Motorcycle Ikon by Diane Spring Slade. 50″ wide, 45″ high, 24″ deep. "Motorcycle ikon, motorcycle psych-on . . ." the artist begins an accompanying poem about worship of the machine. Photographer, ernst.

right: Cosimo by Sharon Lynch. Costumes designed for advertisements and movies include soft sculptured sections for a futuristic look. Photographer, Cosimo.

Running Fench (detail) by William Thielen. 86″ wide, 86″ tall, 20″ deep. Simple materials, dyed muslin, and paper tubing, can make strong sculpture. Photographer, Jeff Newberry.

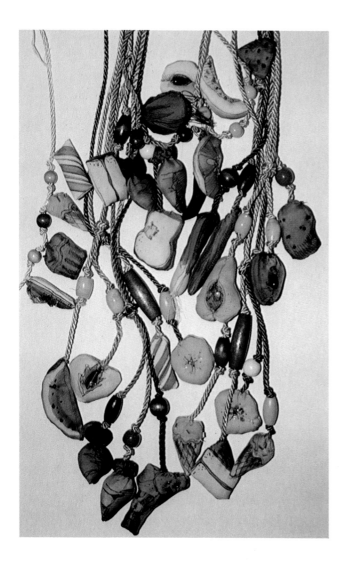

left: Silk Food Belts by Sara Drower. 48″ long. Various soft sculptured snacks hang from cords to be worn around the waist or neck. Permanent dyes are painted and drawn on silk, then set, sewn, stuffed, and sprayed with fabric protector (silicone). Photographer, the artist.

below: Handscape by Ann Nicholson. 42½″ wide, 40¾″ high. Cotton work gloves dyed with procion dyes and stitched to a background create an all over texture of stuffed forms. Colors range from blue to red, diminishing in intensity from bottom to top. Photographer, the artist.

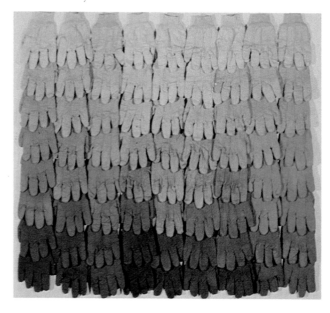

opposite top left: Skunk Cabbage by Sally Cooley. 18″ wide, 12″ high, 2″ thick. The artist uses paint on cotton fabric stuffed with fiberfill to "practice reality." Photographer, the artist.

opposite top right: Parakeet, Peanuts, Ukulele, and Cookies by Susan Bird Kittredge. 15″ wide, 19″ tall. "Each object is appliquéd and stuffed; three-dimensional pieces are sewn to the collage. A wide variety of cotton fabric is assembled by machine sewing." From *Effective English Grade 5*. c. 1979 Silver Burdett Co. Reproduced by permission of Silver Burdett Co.

opposite left: Accordian by Karen Reese. 6′ wide, 6′ high, 6″ thick. Clear vinyl tubes display their various stuffings. Photographer, William Tunnell. Owner, Storehouse, Inc.

right: Portrait by Jo Ellen Trilling. 27″ high by 20″ wide. Fabric, wire, fur, and paint in the hands of a skilled soft sculptor can result in a realistic portrait.

below: Siren by Jappie King Black. 12″ tall. Carefully crocheted sections assemble into an appealing bird creature. The wire armature shows as wrapped legs and feet. Photographer, Richard Black.

left: Head of a Faun by Debora Minsky Jackson. 10″ wide, 20″ tall, 8″ deep. The artist shaped a painted machine embroidered canvas into a sculptured head with pointed green ears and curly Persian lamb hair. Photographer, Bill Guisler.

right: Flower Costume by Silvia Vigiletti. Life-sized. "Arms fit into sleeves with large stuffed leaves attached. Stuffed flower petals form a ring that snaps around the neck. A flat hat of stuffed balls goes on your head for the flower center. You can see out between the flower petals enough. The flower can become a center piece of a pedestal sculpture when not worn." Photographer, Robert Vigiletti.

below: Caladiums Batikimus by Susan McCullough. 18″ wide, 18½″ tall, 13″ wide. The realistically dyed leaves in shades of magenta, green and brown cause many viewer doubletakes because of their authenticity. The batik technique suits this plant portrait ideally. Owner, Arts and Humanities Council of Baton Rouge, La. Photographer, the artist.

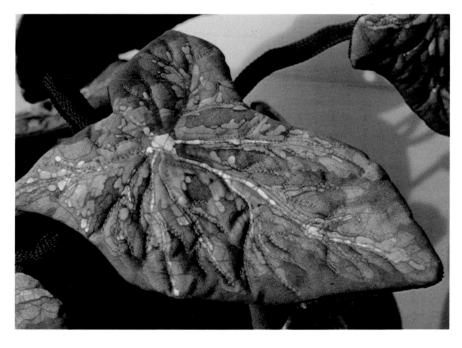

right: Self-Portrait by Lynn DiNino. Life-sized. Paying extraordinary attention to detail allows this artist to make realistic portraits. Photographer, Donn Leber.

below: Shell Collection by Ricki Crusciel. Largest: 18″ wide, 19″ tall, 3″ thick. Shells, first folded fan-shaped, were tie-dyed Kyochi-zome style by direct dye application on 100% cotton muslin. Photographer, Vicki Parker.

right: Cat in progress by the author. 16″ tall from *Nine Cats* series. To make a pattern by measure-and-math, draw a full scale sketch, measure across shapes and multiply by 3.14 to find the circumference. Decide where seams must go (sharp lines drawn on front view), then compute the dimensions of each piece (see text).

below left: Daisy by Jill Frey. 30″ wide, 6′ long, 5″ deep. Gathered balls and tubes appear consistently in soft sculpture, here as a flower stem and center, which is stuffed smocking. Estimating the pattern for this piece by the rules for geometric shapes would succeed very well.

below right: Every Cloud Has A Silver Lining by Alice Leeds. 8′ wide, 8″ deep, 10″ tall. Boxes always beguile artists as containers and objects. This silver lined box, made from metallic coated woven fabric, is machine embroidered and quilted and contains a silver clouds machine embroidered with encouraging messages. Photographer, Doug Long. Owner, Ruth D. Meyers.

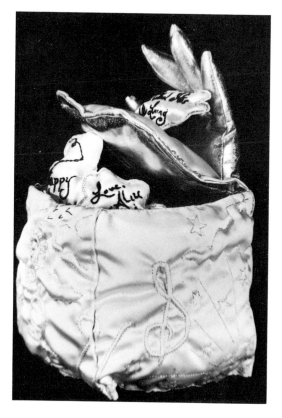

One Piece Pattern

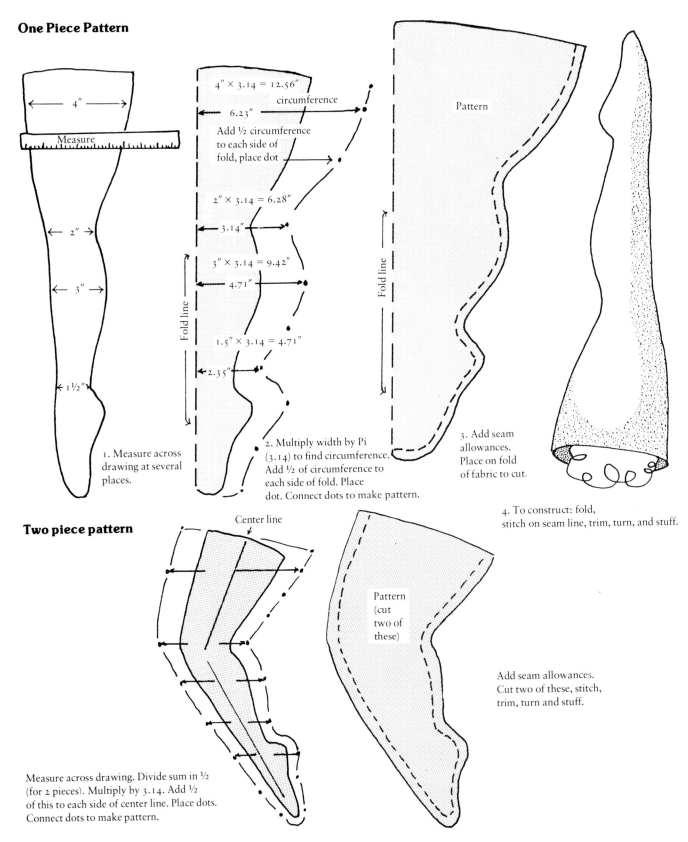

4" × 3.14 = 12.56"
circumference

6.23"

Add ½ circumference
to each side of
fold, place dot

2" × 3.14 = 6.28"

3.14"

3" × 3.14 = 9.42"

4.71"

1.5" × 3.14 = 4.71"

2.35"

4"

Measure

2"

3"

1½"

Fold line

Fold line

Pattern

1. Measure across
drawing at several
places.

2. Multiply width by Pi
(3.14) to find circumference.
Add ½ of circumference to
each side of fold. Place
dot. Connect dots to make pattern.

3. Add seam
allowances.
Place on fold
of fabric to cut.

4. To construct: fold,
stitch on seam line, trim, turn, and stuff.

Two piece pattern

Center line

Pattern
(cut
two of
these)

Measure across drawing. Divide sum in ½
(for 2 pieces). Multiply by 3.14. Add ½
of this to each side of center line. Place dots.
Connect dots to make pattern.

Add seam allowances.
Cut two of these, stitch,
trim, turn and stuff.

Gap and Overlap

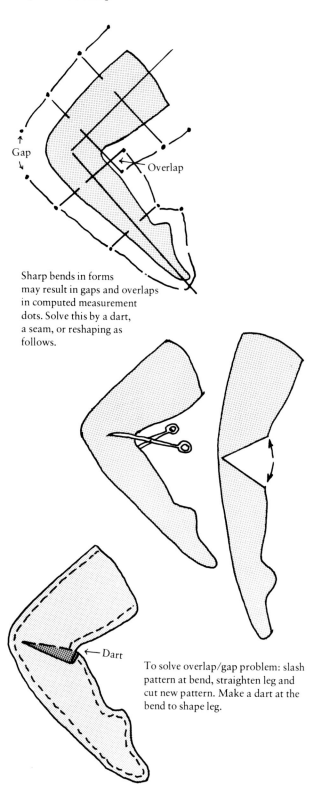

Gap

Overlap

Sharp bends in forms may result in gaps and overlaps in computed measurement dots. Solve this by a dart, a seam, or reshaping as follows.

Dart

To solve overlap/gap problem: slash pattern at bend, straighten leg and cut new pattern. Make a dart at the bend to shape leg.

Measuring Complex Patterns

ESTIMATING FABRIC AMOUNTS

Any pattern you make also shows you how much fabric you need. If you plan to buy fabric before making an accurate pattern, try this method. Make a rough sketch of the object. Decide which of the four basic geometric shapes each part of your figure most closely resembles. Use the rules listed for each geometric shape which tell how much fabric you will need. Add these amounts or sketch these estimated pattern pieces on a diagram to determine how much fabric to buy. Add a little extra for seam allowances, waste in cutting, and a margin of safety.

THE MEASURE AND MATH SYSTEM

This system replaces guessing at pattern shapes with accurate measuring and computing. The same math that measures geometric shapes serves to measure less symmetrical shapes. Since most stuffed shapes fill to roundness, you will use pi or 3.14 the most.

Simply stated, to make any flat drawing into a full round figure, you need to measure across all shapes and multiply by just over three times (3.14) to determine how big around the shapes will be. Measure along outline contours of the drawing to determine the length of seams at that point.

Few figures will be this simple. The complex human figure provides a good example for the types of patterns you may need. These include: the one piece pattern, two piece pattern, the dart, added seams, reshaping, and added pieces.

Begin by making a full sized drawing of the figure you plan. More than one view (front, side, top, etc.) helps to check actual shape. These drawings allow you to measure shapes and then to compare finished stuffed sections for accuracy.

To work from a smaller drawing or photograph, either scale it up to full size by the graph system or multiply your measurements by the necessary number to achieve the size you want. For example, multiply by two for twice the size, by three for three times the size. For a smaller figure, divide in the same manner.

One Piece Pattern

Draw a profile sketch of the figure or part that can be made in one tube-like piece, folded and seamed. (See diagram of legs.) The straight side indicates the fold. Measure across the drawing at the widest, narrowest, and

Adding Seams

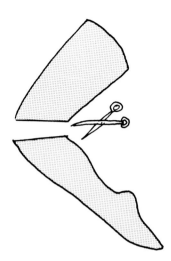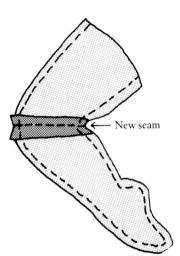

← New seam

Cut pattern at bend. Measure and compute. Add seam allowances all around. Stitch new seam first then assemble.

average places. Multiply each dimension by 3.14. Like the tube, this piece needs to measure more than three times as much around as it is wide.

To make the pattern, place dots outside the drawing at the point of the computed measurement, adding half to each side of the fold line. Connect the dots to make the seam line. This line should measure about the same length as the drawing outline. Add an even ½" to ¾" seam allowance around the edges. The pattern may look odd, but it will be mathematically correct to make the shape drawn.

Two Piece Pattern

Some parts need more shape than a one piece pattern can provide. For example, an arm with a bent elbow needs a seam on each side to create the right shape. To make a two piece pattern, begin with a drawing. Measure across it in several places, the widest, narrowest, and others. Multiply each dimension by 3.14. Divide each computed measurement in half for the two pattern pieces. Draw a line down the center of the arm. Place dots outside the drawing at the point of each computed and divided measurement, adding half to each side of the center line. Add seam allowances. Cut two of these. Be sure to trim seam allowances after stitching to prevent wrinkles.

Gaps and Overlaps

Sometimes more shaping is needed than you can accomplish with one or two pieces. You discover this when computed measurements leave a gap or overlap at corners on your drawing. For example, draw a sharply bent leg. Measure various places as before, multiply by 3.14 and then divide by 2. Place these computed measurement dots at right angles to a mid-line on the drawing. Notice that the dots overlap on the inside of the knee, and leave a

above: Group of Gnomes by Lenore Davis. Figures 25″ tall. Experience as a ceramist helped the artist understand volumes in space. Fabric provides much of the same flexibility for modeling as clay. Photographer, Lenore Davis.

Reshaping

Cut pattern at bend. Pivot piece until computed measurement dots meet. This keeps contours right length. Add seam allowances, then complete. Stuffing will cause leg to bend to right angle.

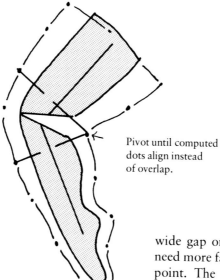

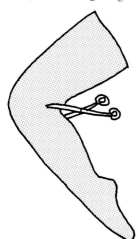

Pivot until computed dots align instead of overlap.

wide gap on the front side. The overlap indicates you need more fabric in the form of a gusset or a seam at this point. The gap means you need a dart, a seam, or reshaping.

Three methods for coping with this problem follow, which you can apply to other sharp corners.

Shape by Dart

Cut out the bent leg drawing you made above. Make a slash at the knee and trace around the leg so it is nearly straight. Compute this new pattern as before. Sew the leg seams on the reverse side. Before you turn it, stitch a dart across the back of the knee to accomplish the bend in the leg. Darts can be used to make bends in any tubular shape.

Adding Seams

Cut the original bent leg pattern into two pieces at the knee. Compute as before to make the pattern, adding a seam allowance to the slashes across the knee. This results in a four piece pattern, two upper and two lower sections. Making additional seams is often the easiest and best answer to getting the shape you want.

Reshaping

Trace the bent leg pattern but do not cut out. Slash behind the knee and straighten the leg. Add paper to fill the open slash, and compute the pattern dots. Swing the pattern into a bent position until the computed contour dots at the back of the knee meet. The contour or outline of a full sized drawing also represents the exact surface measurement or length of a seam appearing there. For this reason contour lines must remain the same length as the drawing for a correct shape. The fully stuffed leg will bend to the position of your drawing.

above: Roxanne by Anne Kingsbury. 24″ tall. Hand stitching in dark threads gives the figure a sutured look as if she might come to life. She calmly wears a creature on her head. Photographer, R. Hildebrand Studio.

right: Man and Box by Chris Carpenter. 18″ wide, 28″ high, 5″ deep. "I developed a technique I call Structural-Stitchery, a method which uses an armature in combination with upholstery and stitching techniques." Here a man struggles with rigid enclosing forms. Photographer, Jeff Newberry.

far right: Male Cadaver by Susan Anson. 18″ wide, 72″ long, 8″ deep. Done as part of her master's degree project, this anatomical dissection study teaches the artist human construction. Shiny, transparent, or canvas materials mimic body textures.

Drum Solo by Marjorie Trout. 40″ wide, 31″ tall, 6″ deep. "Obviously the drummer of a great drum solo has more than two hands! This idea began as a charcoal and ink drawing, then was adapted to fabric and stuffing. I view soft sculpture as a three-dimensional way to draw." Photographer, Buchner & Young.

Solving Pattern Problems

Examine stuffed toys, upholstered furniture, and clothing construction to see how others coped with problems in shaping patterns. Patterns for the same sculpture could be cut in several different ways. In general, you know that sharp corners on soft sculptures will require seams, darts, or added sections. Shapes that change rapidly from narrow to wide may well require more pattern pieces. Places where one section joins another, necks, shoulders, or hips, will need seams or added pattern pieces for stronger construction.

ADDED SECTIONS

Some soft sculptors work as if they built their pieces in clay, adding sections and pieces as needed. This helps to avoid long seams when adding noses, knees, breasts, or bumps. Resulting seams outline the sections.

JOINTS

For flexible joints, arms and legs can be sewn flat to a body shape. Stitching across a tubular arm or leg compresses the stuffing and allows this joint to flex freely.

More solid joints result from round joinings. These three-dimensional joints hold a figure more firmly erect.

CUT AND FIT

The basic technique of measuring and computing, combined with other techniques for shaping, will help to define problems and construct patterns more accurately. However, since each new soft sculpture can present a varied set of problems, you may need to cut and fit experimentally, a method that all soft sculptors use.

 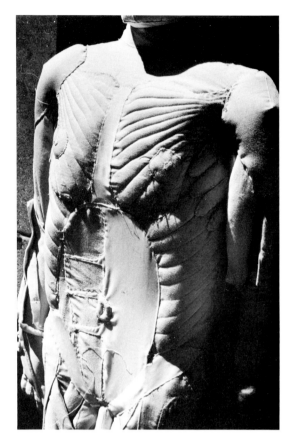

Flexible Joints

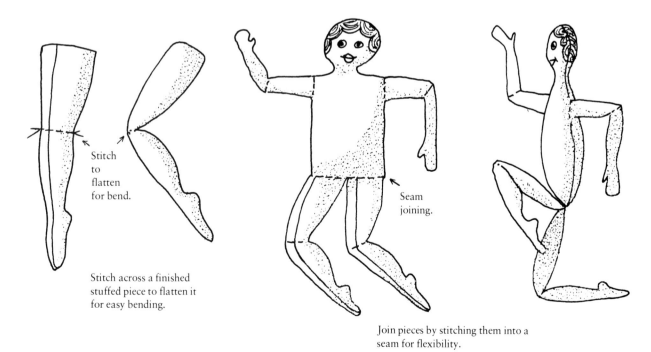

Stitch
to
flatten
for bend.

Stitch across a finished
stuffed piece to flatten it
for easy bending.

Seam
joining.

Join pieces by stitching them into a
seam for flexibility.

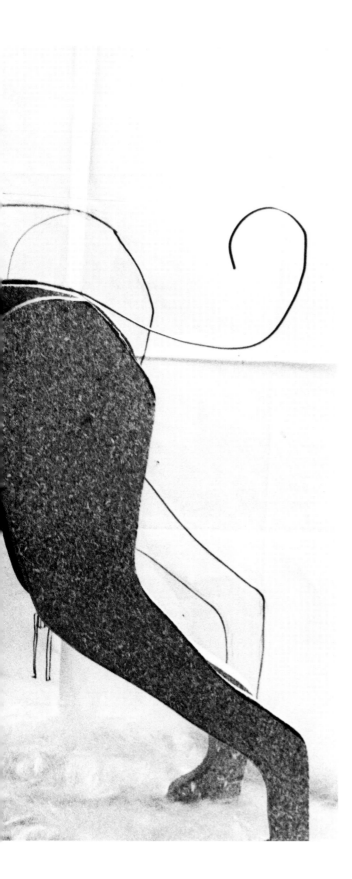

Chapter 7
Armatures

Imagine a giraffe with no bones in his neck. Pretty floppy, right? Armatures, like bones, provide a framework for supporting soft materials. Soft sculpture armatures can be made with an assortment of materials in various ways to solve problems like the giraffe's.

Primarily, frameworks to be covered by stuffing and fabric must be strong enough to support the weight of materials added plus a margin of strength for general wear and tear. Anything the public can touch should be three times stronger than necessary. Whether the armature is large and rigid or minimal and flexible, it will need solid construction and sturdy materials. It takes major surgery to repair the armature inside a soft sculpture.

Types of Armatures

Internal frameworks, like human skeletons, help hold soft sculptures in shape. Some figures need support for only one area: a neck, a leg, an arm, or a tail. In this case, use an unattached armature inserted with the stuffing, such as a wire, a stick, or some tubing.

Some soft sculpture needs a full rigid framework made like upholstered furniture. A sturdy base of wood or metal or even a piece of furniture forms a good base for padding. To build the desired shape, model layers of stuffing on the base, and tie, staple, tack, or sew them in place. Cover the stuffing with a skin of muslin to compress it and to reduce strain on the surface fabric. Heavy or firm external coverings do not need this lining and can be sewn, stapled, nailed, or otherwise affixed directly onto the padded framework. Pad all parts of the armature that might cause lumps in the covering. Sharper forms result when no padding covers the framework and surface material is wrapped, sewn, or stapled directly on the framework.

Exposed frameworks become part of the design. Yarns, fabrics, or soft shapes can be made to cling to the armature by wrapping, sewing, crocheting, macrameing or other means. Artists utilize gravity to create forms in

left: Afghan Dog by the author. A full-sized drawing made from a photograph of a friend's show dog provided a pattern. Armature sections were sawed from three-quarter particle board with a saber saw. The coathanger wire tail was stapled in place; sections were screwed and glued together.

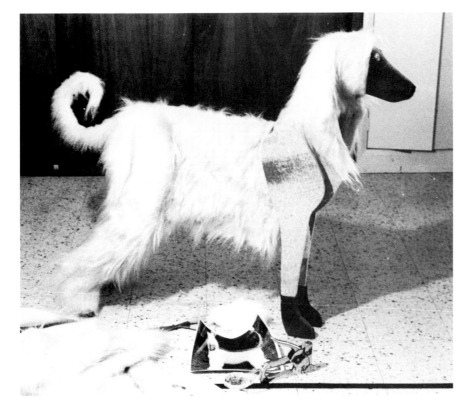

above left: Afghan Dog by the author. 30″ high, 28″ long. Back lighting shows the wispy fur strands of the modacrylic fabric used over the wooden armature for this show dog.

above right: Dog. The head and feet were built up with padding then covered with machine sewn velveteen pieces of fabric. To make machine sewn seams on fur fabrics, brush fur away from the seam so it will not show when turned.

left: Dog. Working from the photograph, large sections of fur were draped and cut in place, then stapled or hand sewn to shape. No additional padding was added to maintain the slender bony look. Metal buttons provided eyes.

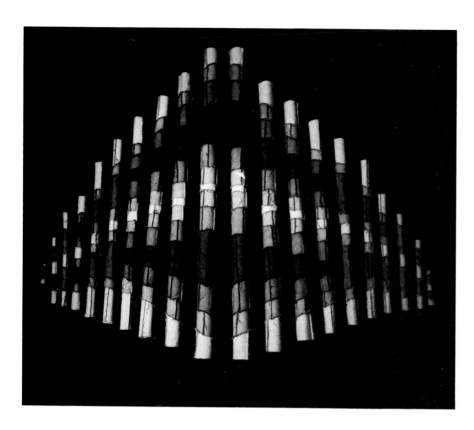

left: Double Running by William Thielen. 6″ to 86″ tall, 36″ deep. Rolled cardboard tubes ranging from 1 to 8 inches in diameter and from 6 to 86 inches high provide a firm lightweight armature for monochromatic dyed muslin fabric with raw edges exposed. Diminishing sizes implies distance and movement. Photographer, Jeff Newberry.

below left: Breast Vest by Rosalie Sherman. 14″ wide, 20″ tall, 14″ deep. Seeing the museum's armor exhibition inspired this sculptor to make a "female suit of armour." The piece maintains its shape by hanging from monofilament lines. Photographer and owner, Minna Resnick.

below center: Totem by Jeanne Boardman Knorr. 24″ wide, 7′ tall, 10″ thick. *Totem*, one of a series done in tribute to the American Indian, consists of an exposed welded steel armature hung with padded forms. Photographer, Phil Morrison.

below right: Three Objects by William Thielen. 9″ wide, 9′ high, 9′ deep. Two wire loop armatures within the unstuffed objects help hold them in shape. The artist finds beauty in exposed and frayed seams, variegated hand dyed color, and simple unpressed muslin fabric. Photographer, Jeff Newberry.

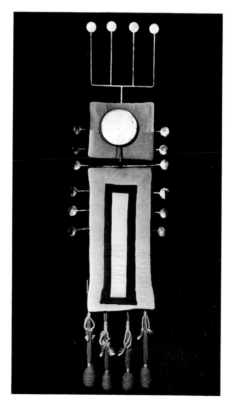

Armatures   75

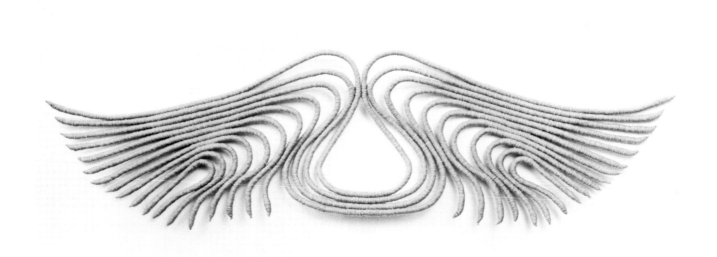

above: Wings by Lillian Ball. 96″ wide, 26″ tall, 6″ deep. Using basketry technique in a sculptural application, the artist wrapped and coiled wool yarns over a rope and wire armature. Photographer, Greg Heins. Owners, Mr. and Mrs. Michael Joblin.

below: Star Ship, Dream Boat by Lillian Ball. 48″ wide, 72″ tall, 10″ deep. The armature allows for designing and constructing large linear pieces.

soft sculptures which hang from a framework. For a more cohesive effect, these exposed frameworks require a surface and shape consistent with their soft materials.

Materials for Armatures

Anything found around the house, from an oatmeal box to a coathanger, might be just what you need for a suitable armature. For large pieces or for special effects, use sturdier materials. Each material listed has different advantages for various requirements.

WIRE

Wire is strong, flexible, and easy to manipulate in the smaller diameters. Untempered wires, such as stove wire, welding rods, or aluminum rods, bend easily. Tempered wires flex but spring back into place unless firmly shaped. These include coat hangers or piano wire. Interlaced wires, such as picture hanging wire, chicken wire fencing, or other fencing wires give good, light weight support. You can model the chicken wire easily by pinching the wires into shape with gloved hands. For more specific shaping, use needle-nosed pliers to crimp wires into

above: Waterfall Trilogy by Lillian Ball. 84″ wide, 72″ long, 4″ deep. Blue and green fabrics stretched on firm backing furnish a solid base for the flow of wool yarns. Photographer, Greg Heins.

below: Sea Theme by Suzi Johnson. 15″ wide, 21″ tall, 15″ deep. Wispy tentacles, stuffed gloves, and other fabric shapes are colored with dyes, felt markers, and resin paint.

shape. Wires work well in combination with other materials. For example, nail, staple, or insert wires into a heavy wooden base for stability.

Other metal supports include: angle irons, braces, stove pipes, tubing, and pipes. If you do not have the facility to weld rods into shape, use plumbing pipes, joints, and elbows which screw together.

WOOD

Wood comes in many forms: dowel rods, boards, plywood sheets, shaped moldings, rough lath, or other building materials from the lumber yard. From home owners' yards come sticks, branches, or logs. Household discards include broomsticks, furniture, spools, tool handles, wooden spoons, popsicle sticks, skewers, or parts of old furniture.

To cut or carve wood, use hobby or woodworking tools, matt knife, dremel tool, saws, drills, or sanders. To assemble wooden parts use screws, nails, large staples, glue, wire, bolts, cord, or whatever holds the parts firmly in place. Many soft sculptors use dowel sticks inserted with the stuffing to hold small figures erect, then drill dowel sized holes in a block of wood base for easy assembly.

Armatures   77

above left: L.I.R.R. Commuter by Jo Ellen Trilling. 9″ long by 12″ high. He's off to the races, this small figure made from fabric, leather, and fur sewn over a wire armature. Photographer, Peter Aaron.

above right: Something Evil by Nancy Gano. 3′ wide, 4′ high, 8″ deep. Tribal masks that ward off evil inspired this wall hanging. Colorful shades of no-wale corduroy are appliquéd and stretched on a shaped Masonite backing. Stuffed shapes added later were stitched on through holes in the Masonite.

left: Fern by Sande Duckworth. 5′ wide, 4″ tall. A framework used for weaving fibers in basketry creates an excellent armature for this piece.

PAPER

Tightly rolled newspapers or laminated cardboard make surprisingly sturdy light weight supports. For large, light weight sculpture, tear paper strips and glue them onto a modeled chicken wire framework. Use several layers for a stronger shell.

OTHER OBJECTS

Any object could give just the kind of support you need: plastic or glass bottles, tin cans, waste baskets, balls, or discarded equipment — an exercise machine, bike parts, lawn sprinkler, skate board, or clothes rack. Styrofoam, which comes as molded packing or sheets of insulations, can easily be cut to shape, and weighs practically nothing.

Small sculptures or parts of large ones may need only the minimal support of stiff fabrics. Stiffeners include canvas, interfacings (Pellon, tailor's canvas), vinyl sheeting, leather, or string wrapped bundles of fabric.

left: Grandma by Susan Slater. Life-size. A papier-mâché core over a chicken wire armature is overlayed with a plaster composition. Melted beeswax and paraffin brushed on give the appearance of flesh. No listing of materials can account for the fragile loneliness the figure projects.

left: Marcel Marceau by Julie Staller-Pentelnik 32″ tall. "I chose Marceau as a subject because mimes, like marionettes, do not communicate verbally." Special solutions are required for movable armatures. Photographer, Dan Kohn.

Reasons for Armatures

Several factors influence the need for armatures in soft sculpture: size, weight, shape, materials, construction, and function or use.

Large pieces will be more apt to need support than small ones. Small sculptures may need only their outer skin and firm stuffing to hold their shape. You will need a sturdier "skin" as size and weight increase and possibly an armature as well.

The weight of a piece itself can cause it to slump. To counter this, diminish weight by using lighter materials and airy construction using as an example a bird's meshwork bones and fluffy feathers.

For more solid pieces, keep elephants in mind. They are designed for carrying their weight with short sturdy legs and thick, tough skin. Compact shapes need an armature less than long protruding pieces or narrow areas between sections. To avoid problems like floppy necks, cut the pattern to include the hair with the neck, make the neck thicker than usual, or cut the pattern to achieve a sturdy round neck shape. Try several drawings of a planned soft sculpture with unwieldy protrusions to see if you can redesign it in sturdier form. A well cut pattern can distribute weight and stress, resulting in increased stability. For example, a round soft sculpture will stay erect better than a narrow one. If you cannot change the shape without spoiling your idea, plan an armature as an integral part of your design.

Loosely woven, knitted, sheer, or light weight fabrics cannot support heavy weights effectively. Shifting or heavy stuffings also require extra support. To use these materials, line fragile fabrics with firmer fabrics, use heavy stuffing only to weight the base for stability, and/or use an armature to take the load off the covering.

left: Tasmanian Devil Candy Dish by Lynn DiNino. 12″ high, 10″ wide, 17″ deep. Have a piece of candy, if you dare. "To surpass the stuffed animal label, fabric animals must have a function." So the artist stretched fabric over a wire armature and fitted a plastic dish in his mouth.

right: Alice by Rosalie Sherman. 16″ wide, 22″ tall, 38″ deep. "My dog, Alice, looks like a creature in a doggie suit. I can unzip and unsnap her skin off her plywood frame and send it to the cleaners."

Chapter 8
Surface Design

Throughout history people embellished their fabrics or leathers with designs for richer effect. Indonesians raised dyeing to a distinctive art with their batik, ikat, and block prints. Orientals of earlier cultures dyed silk strands rich colors to embroider elegant, intricate designs on their robes. In addition to breathtaking beauty, these designs designated rank and imparted religious significance.

American Indians beaded, painted, quilled, laced, or wrapped their leather clothing and containers for spiritual meaning and for visual delight. From the Pre-Columbian Peruvians, who created incredible weavings, to our own American stitchers decorating their blue jeans, embroidering needlepoint, piecing quilts, and creating fiber art, all cultures have developed favorite techniques for creating surface designs.

People from the individual artist to the technical staff at fabric mills work constantly to invent new ways to embellish fabric. Soft sculptors create imagery on fabric in three major ways: (1) by sewing, (2) by applying objects, and (3) by adding color.

Embroidery

HAND EMBROIDERY

Embroidery now enjoys a popularity which ebbs and flows but always comes back. More than 300 hand embroidery stitches have been developed. Surprisingly, all can be formed by one or more of four techniques: straight stitches, loop stitches, knot stitches, or couching.

Embroidery divides into several major categories: crewel, needlepoint, quilting, and creative stitchery to name a few. Soft sculptors use a variety of embroidery techniques to design the surfaces of three-dimensional pieces or build the embroidery itself into a three-dimensional low relief.

MACHINE EMBROIDERY

Embroidery by sewing machine differs from hand-sewn embroidery in stitch formation and appearance. Straight stitching, zigzag, or pre-programmed patterned stitches

left: Nine Cats series (6 of 9) by the author. All 16″ tall. Each cat has a different surface treatment and color range, from crewel embroidery, beading, dyeing, appliqué, to sewn on floss strips.

above left: Bag of Groceries by Joan Pasman. 16″ tall, 14″ wide, 7″ deep. Two of the artist's favorite foods appear, embellished with satin stitch hand embroidery and the backstitch for thinner lines.

above right: Nine Cats series (detail). The loose twill weave body fabric allows the blunt tapestry needle to sew easily between strands. The large needle hole permits the use of large yarns. The formation of the running chain (top) and the feather stitch are shown.

decorate fabrics with regular or special sewing machine threads. Threads too big to fit through the needle may be used on the bobbin or "couched" in place with regular threads.

Free motion stitching delights artists because of its freedom of movement. To do this on your machine, begin by easing the pressure on the presser foot. If this is not possible, use an embroidery (darning) foot. This allows for moving the fabric freely in any direction without having to turn it for corners. Disengage the feed dogs (the little serrated feet that move the fabric forward) or set them for no forward movement. Set the machine for straight or zigzag, and thread it with regular or machine embroidery thread. Place your hands on the fabric on either side of the needle. Your hands act as a sewing hoop to keep the fabric flat and to guide movement. Move the fabric as if the needle were a stationary pencil for a fluid line or solid embroidery. Read your machine instruction manual for additional information under "embroidery" or "darning."

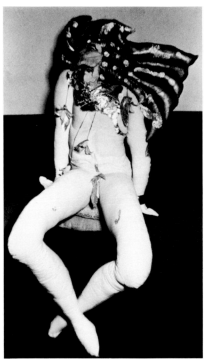

above: Burne Jones Sun Sprite by Debora Minsky Jackson. 24" wide, 6' high, 36" deep. Science fiction stories and an Edward Burne Jones painting inspired this fantasy figure. Metallic fabrics appliquéd to the white background fabric are quilted and machine embroidered for detail. Photographer, Ira Merritt.

right: Pieriot (detail) by Debora Minsky Jackson. Full figure 5' tall. The artist draws with the zigzag sewing machine stitch, coloring in solid areas with directional textured stitching in varied colors. The embellished fabric is then stitched and stuffed into a sculptured form. Photographer, Ira Merritt.

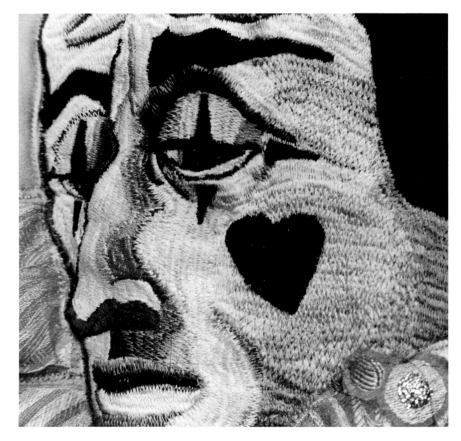

above: The Group by Kathy Murphy. 32" wide, 23" high, 2" deep. Friends at a party stay forever when immortalized in a quilted scene, trapunto stuffed. This machine stitched piece was inspired by a photograph.

below: Garbage Can by Lynn Kartiganer. Life-sized. The quilted gray fabric garbage can contains several carefully constructed flattened tin cans symbolic of short lived vulnerability. Fabric wet with acrylic paint molded over the flattened cans hardened into facsimiles.

Quilting and Trapunto

Quilting alters the fabric surface in two ways. The quilting stitches that bind the face fabric, padding and backing layers together create a decorative line on the fabric. This effect is achieved particularly if the thread and face colors contrast or if the quilting stitches are either embroidered or satin stitched. Secondly, these lines compress the layers producing an appealing puffy fullness in the surrounding areas.

In trapunto, the quilter stuffs some areas with additional padding for increased dimension. Fabrics with surface sheen and minimal pattern look especially effective treated this way.

above left: Little Red Ridinghood by Marcella Marschel. 44″ wide, 82″ long, 6″ deep. The main characters in this drama can be unsnapped or pulled out of pockets on the quilt to replay the scene. The front of Grandmother's house rolls down to conceal her. Characters and quilt are stuffed with fiberfill with appliquéd detailing.

above right: Indian Princess detail by Susan Aaron Taylor. Hand embroidered quilting forms combine with clear vinyl appliqué pockets to form the halo around the Indian Princess (not shown). Photographer, Harry Taylor.

below: Crowning Glory by Doreen Lah. 18″ wide, 10″ tall, 12″ deep. Machine appliqué designs in rich fabrics articulate the two interlocking forms which make one sculpture in puzzle fashion.

Appliqué

Bits and pieces of fabric stitched to another fabric are called "appliqué," a French word for "apply." Appliqué pieces made of non-fraying fabrics need not be hemmed since the hand or machine embroidery around the edges holds them firmly in place.

To machine appliqué, draw a design on fabric and pin it to the backing, then sew around the edge line with close stitches. Trim away the excess fabric. Cover the raw cut edge and the stitch line with machine satin stitching. Appliqué pieces can be stuffed, predecorated, or trimmed before being stitched into place. Different edging stitches accomplish novel effects.

above: Cat (detail). *Nine Cats* series by the author. Orange, purple, metallic gold, and transparent colored beads in different shapes and sizes form a variety of patterns on the fabric surface.

above left: Jewelry by Leslie Masters. 1″ to 5″ across. The soft earrings, necklaces, and pins glow with bright colored satins, sequins, and beads.

Beading

Beads, popular for generations for decoration, come in a variety of materials, sizes, shapes, and kinds: for example, glass, wood, metal, shell, ivory, seeds, paper, gem stones, and plastic. American Indian bead work uses the small glass seed bead.

Beading decoration can be woven on a loom, strung on threads to form netting, or sewn directly to a background. These background materials require two qualities: ease of sewing and a surface texture consistent with the beads. Soft leathers, velvets, wools, silks, and other fine fabrics make beading time worthwhile.

To sew beads to fabric use the spot stitch (one bead at a time), the whip stitch (three or more), or the couching stitch (see diagram). Use fine strong threads that will not break but will fit through the tiny wire needles used for beading. Wax the thread for easy sewing.

Beading Techniques

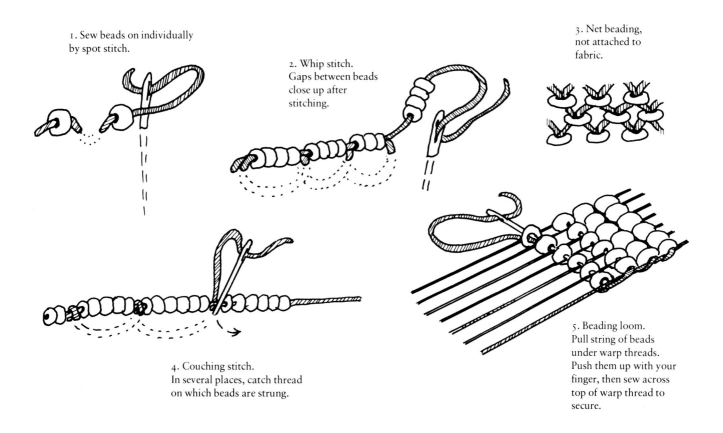

1. Sew beads on individually by spot stitch.

2. Whip stitch. Gaps between beads close up after stitching.

3. Net beading, not attached to fabric.

4. Couching stitch. In several places, catch thread on which beads are strung.

5. Beading loom. Pull string of beads under warp threads. Push them up with your finger, then sew across top of warp thread to secure.

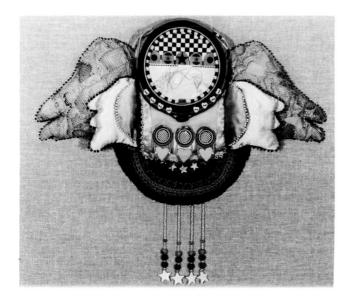

left: Soft Wall Sculpture by Jean Battles-Irvin. 30″ wide, 22″ tall, 1″ thick. With Victorian delight, this stitcher assembles varied objects into one composition. She creates beads, buttons, and bows by many methods: macrame, crochet, wrapping, stuffing, and tatting. Photographer, Stan T. Irvin.

above left: Angel with Red Boots by Lenore Davis. 35" wide, 36" tall, 1" depth. Diminished color in other areas emphasizes the bright red dye painted boots on this quilted figure. Elsewhere, dye color fills in the background to bring out the white forms. Photographer, Lenore Davis. Owner, Permanent Collection, Fine Arts Museum of the South, Mobile, Alabama. Gift of the Art Patrons League in memory of Genevieve H. Owen.

above right: Running Fench by William Thielen. 86" wide, 86" tall, 20" deep. Simple materials, dyed muslin, and paper tubing, can make strong sculpture. See color section for detail. Photographer, Jeff Newberry.

left: Vegetable Vest by Sara Drower. Dye painted stars and moon were machine quilted, stitched, and stuffed, then hung by corded fabric on the vest.

Dyes

Dyes allow you to achieve specific desired colors on fabrics. Dye color particles differ in size and type from those of paint. Paints coat the fabric. Dyed color penetrates the fibers or reacts chemically to become part of the fiber. Dyes leave fibers and fabrics naturally soft with no stiffening.

"Home" dyeing can be an easy process if you use natural fibers, cotton, linen, silk, and wool, and use commercially prepared dyes. Synthetic fibers usually require complex chemistry to dye them.

Be sure to use proper safety precautions when handling and mixing dyes. Work in a ventilated room and wear rubber gloves, apron and a mask when necessary.

Home dyes, sold in powder or liquid form, dissolve in hot water. Add vinegar to set the color in wool and silk; salt to set the color in cotton and linen. Dip fabrics in the dye bath for light colors, agitate and simmer for deeper ones. You may also need to add more dye or overdye to deepen color. Wash out all extra dye with cool water. These dyes are not as bright or permanent as the fiber reactive type.

above: *Caladiums Batikimus* by Susan McCullough. 18″ wide, 18½″ tall, 13″ wide. The realistically dyed leaves in shades of magenta, green and brown cause many viewer doubletakes because of their authenticity. The batik technique suits this plant portrait ideally. Owner, Arts and Humanities Council of Baton Rouge, La. (See detail in color section).

below: *Shell* by Susan McCullough. Largest: 8″ wide, 5″ high, 4″ deep. "It's time consuming to batik the fabric first but worth the effort for the unique results."

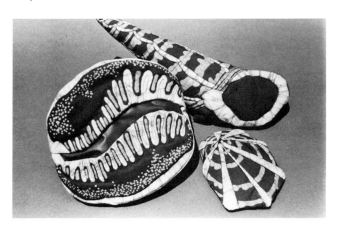

Fiber reactive dyes, such as procion dyes, require a mordant to activate chemical bonding. A typical recipe calls for 2 parts urea, 2 parts soda, ¼ part dye, ⅛ part resist salt, 10 parts water. Boil the fabric with washing soda before dyeing to make it clean and receptive. The dye mixture need not be hot and will complete its dye action in about an hour. These clear, bright colors must be set in sun, air, or steam heat, or by pressing.

DYE PAINTINGS

Use procion dyes for brilliance and permanence. Add thickener to the dyes for a better paint consistency. Dye the pieces of a soft sculpture before you stitch them together since seams resist dyeing. Stretch the fabric taut to paint. Slightly damp fabrics may accept dye more readily. Painted lines tend to diffuse like wet watercolor painting as dye follows the fibers.

After the first dyeing of one or more colors, set the colors, wash out the extra dye, and highlight your design with a second application of dye paint. For more specific information, read the directions that come with the dyestuffs.

TIE-DYE

The following simple resist technique allows you to achieve a design easily. Fold or tightly tie dampened fabric in various places so the dye will not penetrate. For example, tie a string around pebbles for small circles, create an accordian fold for stripes, or clamp wood on folds or gathers for other patterns. Use only hot water direct dyes for this method. For the clearest patterns, wash out the residual dye before untying the strings. Retie and overdye for more elaborate patterns.

BATIK

In this technique, wax or a resist paste prevents dye from reaching waxed areas of the fabric. Typically, hot beeswax mixed with paraffin is painted, block printed, or trailed onto the fabric. Since hot water would melt the wax, the waxed fabric goes into a cold dye bath (procion dyes). If the batik is crumpled before dyeing, the characteristic crackle will appear in the waxed areas. Boil the dyed piece to set procion colors and to remove excess wax. Wax may also be removed by turpentine or by ironing between sheets of paper. Heat from ironing also helps set color. Repeat the process for added colors. Overdying colors results in new colors. For example, blue over yellow makes green, and orange over green makes brown.

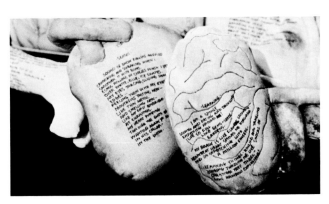

top left: Scene by Leslie Masters. 48″ wide, 72″ tall, 12″ deep. To change the weather to your liking just choose which star, moon, or cloud to hang in the sky. All shapes are painted with artist's acrylic on canvas, then sewn over the stuffing, unturned.

top right: Portrait Box by Gail Molnar. 10″ high, 8″ wide, 8″ deep. Permanent ink outlines the self-portrait stitched on the box lid. The emerging, stuffed organs are colored realistically.

bottom right: Portrait Box (detail). Poetry, appropriate to the function and feeling of each organ, is inscribed with ink on their acrylic painted surfaces. The heart poem describes "senses" and the brain poem "learning."

bottom left: Sgt. Pepper by Dee Durkee. 10″ tall. "Beatles" characters play their painted instruments with enthusiastic gestures. The muslin figures are first firmly stuffed, undercoated with white paint, then completed with bright waterproof acrylic paint.

Adding Color

PAINT

Painters can use fabric soft sculpture forms like shaped canvas. Most choose acrylic paint for its tough, flexible waterproof surface and bright color. On uncoated fabric, acrylic diffuses softly and acts as a ground for added color. Firmly stuffed pieces, prepared with a ground of glue sizing and gesso or undercoat paint, give a hard clean surface for crisp lines and bright colors.

Textile paints, oil paints, and water proof inks also adhere well to fabrics. Impermanent watercolor paint or ink smears when touched.

MARKING PENS

It is unfortunate that permanent marking pens are not fast color since they are wonderfully easy to use for embellishing soft sculpture. These dyes may migrate along fabric fibers, fade in sunlight, or transfer to other fabrics. However, just for fun, use them anyway.

above: Gare by the author. Life-sized. Natural colored cotton and polyester muslin fabric is stitched and stuffed into a five year old boy-sized figure. Tennis shoes are real, the face is drawn on with permanent ink.

below: Rhinoceros by Ruth Roberts. 34″ long, 24″ high. These lines can be drawn with a magic marker or with a pen or brush dipped in dye or ink, with a tjanting used for trailing wax in batik. These lines and colors are made with procion dyes. Photographer, John Russell.

PRINTING

Printed designs, done with thickened dyes, screen printing inks, or other paints, achieve more uniform color and sharper edges than dye painting. Printing techniques range from simple block printing that children can manage to screen printing, a stencil technique that allows for intricate detail. A "silk screen" consists of a frame stretched with a fine mesh of silk, nylon, wire mesh, or organdy. Blocked out areas prevent screen-printing ink from printing. The print appears when ink poured onto the screen is forced through the open areas in the design by a squeegee pulled across it. Designs can be made and applied to the screen in several ways: cut out of film, painted on with Block-Out (a liquid glue), or stuck on the screen impermanently. Each color needs a screen in a multi-colored design.

above: Scallops by Joan Lintault. 20″ wide, 18½″ long, 11″ deep. Modern technology allows for printing a color slide by xerography on transfer paper. This image can transfer to many surfaces including fabric, shown here. Airbrushed colors further enrich the surface, which is then quilted, shaped, and stuffed.

Photographic Techniques

The magic realism of photographic imagery can be applied to fabric in several ways. In screen printing, the image or a film line positive of it (black image on clear film) is exposed by sunlight or arc lamp onto a light sensitive gel. The processed gel blocks out non-printing areas when adhered to the screen and printed.

A light-sensitive solution can be painted or dipped onto the fabric itself. By this means, the photograph is exposed and developed directly on the fabric. Images also may be blue-printed onto a fabric or printed on transfer paper by color xerography and then applied. The most direct method for using photographs is to sew, laminate, or glue them to the fabric surface.

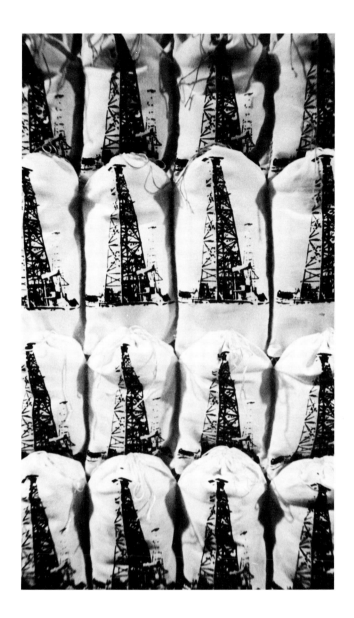

above left: To the Winter of 74 by Sidney Wilson. Each bag 4″ by 6″. Each muslin bag, screen printed with the Texas symbol of the oil derrick, is stitched in rows to a backing to form a large wall hanging. The repeated forms become an overall texture.

left: Book of Ruth by Alice Leeds. 13″ wide, 15″ tall, 1″ thick. Machine sewn pages, including the photographs, unfold accordian style on quilted pages.

above right: London Bus by Claudia Hall. 12″ wide, 12″ high, 4″ deep. The London bus photograph is appliquéd to muslin backing, which stretches over the box. A translucent backing on the box allows light to come through the Kodalith (positive print on clear film) photograph of London bobbies inside. From the *15 Boxes* series.

Chapter 9
Constructions

Fabric Constructions

If it seems we have covered all ways of making soft sculpture, consider the techniques of fabric construction. Fiber artists weave, macrame, knit, crochet, make lace or felt, or mix fiber and fabric to make soft sculpture.

Construction of soft sculpture or fiber objects depends strongly on the nature of the materials used. Greater knowledge of materials leads to more inventiveness. The techniques used to construct objects also influence the final form strongly. For example, knitting stretches while knotting holds firmly.

KNIT/STOCKING FIGURES

Knitted fabric stretches freely in all directions due to its construction. Hand and simple machine knitting consists of one continuous strand looped to the next row of loops. Making knitted "stocking" figures fascinates and delights many soft sculptors because the process resembles modeling with clay.

To make these stocking doll figures, choose flesh tone nylon stockings or any finely knit fabric. The flexibility of knit fabrics diminishes the need for seams, so cut simple patterns. Sew most seams by machine for strength since knits stretch and run. To prevent this, use the small zigzag stitch or stretch stitch. Sew over paper backing for support. The needle perforates the paper for easy removal.

Model the face, body, and hand details by hand sewing. First stuff the figure firmly with fiberfill or other soft non-shifting fiber. To make a nose shape protrude, secure the thread end with a hidden knot, then insert the needle on one side of the nose. Poke it under the required amount of stuffing then bring the needle out the other side of the nose. Pull the thread tightly enough to lump up the stuffing. Continue to stitch under and across the nose until you have modeled the nose shape.

To make dimples, nostril or eye sockets, insert the needle on the back of the head or some hidden place and

left: Five Friends Celebrating the Kurtz' 50th Anniversary by Barbara Johansen Newman. 22″ wide, 18″ high. This artist creates remarkably skillful and lively portraits by needle, thread, fiberfill stuffing, and stretchy knit fabrics. Owner, I. Sigman.

above left: With Pepperoni by Barbara Johansen Newman. 22″ high. One fabulous pizza painted, quilted, and embroidered, coming up! Photographer, Harvey Ferdschneider. Owner, I. Sigman.

above right: Father's Night In by Joan Schulze. 8″ wide, 12″ high, 14″ long. This whimsical hand-sewn nylon stocking figure completely fills the satin lined stuffed tub with shell feet. "This is a portrait of my father."

knot the thread. Push the needle through, emerging at the dimple or eye. Reinsert the needle a few strands away and pull needle out the back. Pull thread until the dimple is deep enough, then secure the thread. If necessary, add stuffed pieces for lips, eye lids, noses, or fingers. Soft knit fabric will most likely need an armature for support.

To complete the figure, use anything that suits; acrylic paint drybrushed on like rouge for color, seed pearls for gleaming teeth, or buttons or embroidery for eyes. For hair use wig trimmings, unspun wool, yarn, or whatever creates the desired effect. Attach hair so it covers the modeling stitching on the back of the head. Keep clothing in scale for those petite people. Quarter sized figures need quarter scale fabrics to look right.

READY MADE CLOTHING

At some time most soft sculptors try making a piece all or in part from ready made clothing. The clothing consists

above: Time Out by Ann Watson. 36″ wide, 16″ high, 22″ deep. This denim figure shows the gamut of hand work techniques: embroidery, knitting, crochet, hand and machine stitching, and stuffing. The painted satin pretzels have French knot embroidered salt. Photographer, Joe A. Watson.

left: Starter Plant Seller by Georgia Landau. 27″ tall. Soft sculptors can surround themselves with their friends by making portraits of them.

of interesting patterns, colors, or fabrics. It also carries the aura of the wearer, for example, a beaded flapper dress, a military uniform, a football jersey, work gloves, or blue jeans.

FOLDS AND GATHERS

All techniques used to make clothing or household furnishings also apply to soft sculpture. For example, folding, gathering, and ruffling accomplish a three-dimensional effect without stuffing. Folds, pleats, wrinkles, or tucks can be stitched in place by hand or machine. Experiment by folding paper since layers and folds of paper closely resemble fabric. Folded bands of fabric, stitched fabric tubing, or ribbon may be used like yarn for plaiting, braiding, knotting, or crocheting on an increased scale. You can stitch pieces handled in these ways to a background fabric to resemble a flossa rug or heavily textured surface.

above left: Angel Costume by Diane Spring Slade. 48″ wing span. Fascinated with the concept of angels, wings, and their symbolism, the artist first made this as a Halloween costume, then stuffed it as a wall hanging.

above right: High Chair by Alice Leeds. 16″ wide, 50″ tall, 18″ deep. The artist makes a play on words by making a player into a chair. "High Chair is a tall, brown velvet basketball player, wearing sneakers on his feet." From her *18 Chairs* series. Photographer, Joseph Yarzzo.

below: A Persuasion of Pleats by B. J. Adams. 18″ wide, 14″ high, 1″ deep. This imaginative wall hanging takes advantage of the natural fold, drape, and flexibility of fabric. Pleats are pressed firmly, then stitched in place. Photographer, Clark G. Adams.

Fiber Constructions

MACRAME

Macrame objects consist of a series of knots, usually tied tightly enough to give dimensional stability to the finished piece. No loom is necessary. Two basic knots, the half knot and the half hitch, are used in endless variations. Tools needed include: scissors, pins, ruler, knotting board, rings, tapestry needles, and crochet hooks.

To macrame, you will need the right number of cords, measured 3½ to 4 times the length of the finished piece. Double this cord length to make two "ends." To begin, knot the cords on a holding cord, ring, stick, or other base. Build the piece by tying knots firmly and close to the previous one (unless directions say otherwise). Follow a geometric design or work randomly.

Macrame, when worked tightly, does not need an armature to maintain its three-dimensional shape. Macrame often resembles weaving, crochet, or wrapping depending on the knot patterns.

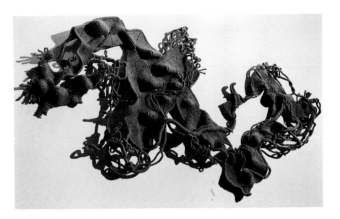

above left: Double Loop Knot by Joan Michaels-Paque. 6" wide, 24" high, 2" deep. This knitted and knotted sculpture is based on a study of topology, how some surfaces remain the same through bending or stretching. Photographer, Henry P. Paque.

above right: Transcendental Tendencies by Joan Michaels-Paque. 9' 3" wide, 3½' tall, 11" thick. Based on her knowledge of topology and structure in nature and art, this macrame artist builds a self-sustaining form by knotting, weaving, and wrapping synthetic fibers that need no armature. Photographer, Henry P. Paque. Owner, Guaranty Savings.

below right: Horizon Line by Becky Clark. 72" wide, 36" high, 3" deep. In the most understated minimalist terms, this artist subtly articulates a three-dimensional knotted surface in color. Photographer, Jeffrey Clark.

below left: Dusk to Midnight by Becky Clark. 30" wide, 40" high, 4" deep. Subtle color changes carry out the theme. Knotted panels are turned on themselves and stitched together to form the dimensional relief. Photographer, Jeffrey Clark.

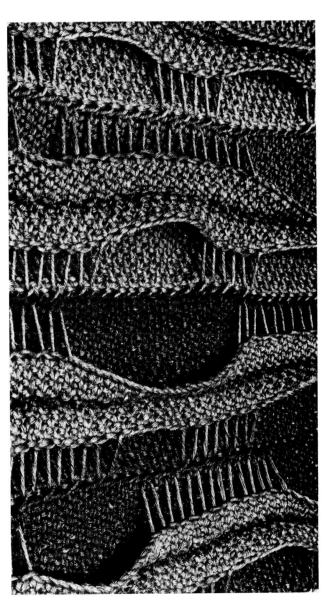

above: Dream Boat (detail) by Lillian Ball. Bundles of wool strands wrapped tightly form sturdy upright stalks that need no armatures. Photographer, Greg Heins. Owner, Mr. and Mrs. Ronald Sholom.

below: Emergence From Yellow by Jeanne Boardman Knorr. 24″ wide, 36″ high, 24″ deep. Fibers twisted into strands, strands twisted into yarns, yarns twisted into ropes, ropes wrapped into forms — the piece grows in logical progression to completion.

WRAPPING

Wrapping a central core with another fiber achieves several appealing results. It decorates the surface, increases the core size, and stiffens the center core. Use any fiber from matching tones to lustrous silk threads to loose woolly ones to wrap the center core. Grass, raffia, wire, or ribbon give different effects.

Wrapped cords become quite firm and may well stand alone. Use several layers to build a sculptural form. Keep the core fiber taut, wrap firmly and neatly, and secure ends of wrapping in an unobtrusive manner. Wrapping can be combined with other techniques.

WEAVING

Although most soft sculptors use commercially woven fabrics for construction, many succeed in weaving three-dimensional forms on the loom. Basic weaving consists of warp yarns strung on the loom, interlaced with weft or filler yarns woven across the warp. Weavers accomplish endless variation by the use of certain types of looms, different weaves, kinds of yarn, and means of construction.

As in other fabric construction techniques, the weaver must keep the warp thread yarns taut, prevent the weft yarns from tangling (often by winding the yarns on a shuttle which carries the weft through the separation of warp yarns called the "shedd") and maintain a consistent hand for even weaving.

Contemporary weavers build three-dimensional forms by double weaving, resulting in a hollow tube, by tapestry weaving, or by any manner of weaving sections that can be assembled off the loom.

BASKETRY

Basket woven soft sculptures scarcely resemble containers. These complex forms result from a variety of basketry techniques: coiling, weaving, twining, and other variations.

Coiled baskets grow in a spiral fashion, with the core yarn wrapped to an adjacent yarn by an auxiliary strand. Woven baskets result from interlacing strands. The warp may consist of a framework of stiffer fibers, with the more flexible weft fibers woven across or in a continuous spiral. Twined baskets twist two yarns around the warp in a manner similar to weaving.

Archaeologists find solid evidence that baskets appeared before clay containers developed. With so many thousands of years of background you can imagine how many different ways exist to make baskets.

Unlike most weaving, coiling, twining, or weaving a

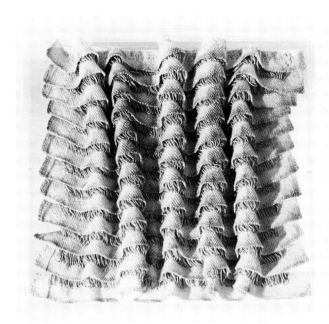

above: Sensitivities by Lesley Shearer. 13½″ wide, 12¼″ high, 2″ deep. "I want the work to be from the loom, but not of the loom." This weaver aims to make the result more interesting than the process of weaving, and experiments with three-dimensional images. Photographer, E. Ann Hunt.

right: Trees by Janet Goldner. 8′ tall. The dividing line between weaving and basketry comes not from technique but equipment. No loom is used in basket weaving.

below: Sea Quilt by Susan Bird Kittredge. 62″ wide, 63″ high, 4″ deep. Fabric strips, stuffed with fiberfill, are coiled then sewn together to build three-dimensional forms.

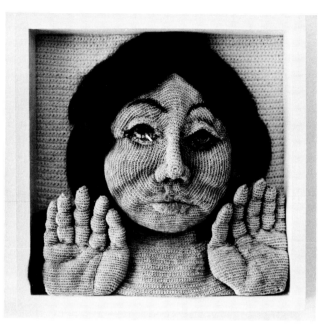

left: Boxed In by Jappie King Black. 12″ wide, 5′ 6″ tall. This female nude, partitioned by boxes, is crocheted in varying flesh tones, as evidenced by the bathing suit marks. Photographer, Richard Black.

above: Boxed In (detail of face). The crocheted lines spiraling around the face give the sensation of vertigo. Crocheted forms were stitched, stuffed, and embellished with paint and yarns. Photographer, Richard Black.

below: Boxed In (detail 12″ square foot box). Look into the mirror under the crocheted stuffed feet and you too become boxed in. Photographer Richard Black.

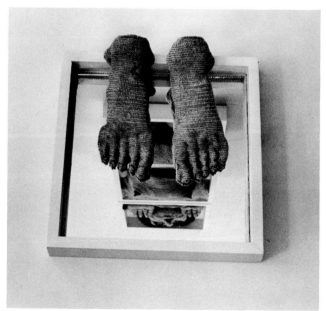

above left: Mermaid by Jane Reiter. 12″ high. Just unzip the mermaid tail and out steps a shapely crocheted lady. You knew all along that's how it works, didn't you?

above right: Leo by the author. 16″ tall, *Nine Cats* series. Shades of brown, gold, and white yarns spiral around the soft fiberfill stuffing to form the cat. Front legs are stiffened with dowel stick armatures; the nose is embroidered.

Coiling

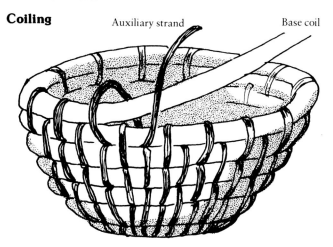

Auxiliary strand   Base coil

In one of many coiling techniques, an auxiliary strand wraps around the base cord, securing it to the adjacent base cord in the coiled form.

basket does not require a loom. The basket maker freely constructs any shape the materials can support. Even soft flexible materials, when combined with more rigid ones or worked tightly, become firm enough to hold a shape.

CROCHET

Crocheted fabric or forms consist of a continuous row of looped knots that unravel only if the last knot is not secured. This fabric expands slightly if loosely done or stretchy yarns are used but does not stretch like knitting. Use any combination of the three variables to achieve different effects: (1) different sized crochet hooks, (2) different type, size, and color of yarns, and (3) different stitches and patterns. Tightly knotted crocheting of firm threads may make a self-supporting figure but you will probably need an armature or very firm stuffing for most.

FELTING

The newest direction in fiberforms resurrects the ancient technique of felting. According to stories, nomads put a layer of unspun wool under the camel's saddle. The interaction of heat, moisture, pressure, and movement, and the scaley cell structure of wool, matted the wool into felt. Felters combine the same elements today except the camel may be replaced with a washer and dryer, or other modern devices.

above left: Linear Transition by Lida Gordon. 17″ wide, 27″ tall, 1″ deep (each unit). Handmade felt is combined with gauze to make these relief sculptures. Photographer, Bill Gillis.

above right: Nevada Highway by Barbara Chover. 3′ wide, 3′ high, 3′ deep. This felted scene sits on a platform and hangs on the wall. Stuffed three-dimensional mountains sit at the fold. Felted wool and unspun silk clouds are all vegetable dyed. Photographer, the artist.

below left: Felt Baskets by Rosalie Shirley. 6″ to 8″ in diameter. Handmade felt baskets, formed over a mold, incorporate various materials: jute, linen, baling twine, and reindeer hair, within the wool batt. Photographer, Ken Heywood.

above left: Fences and Other Barriers by Linda Johnson. 58″ wide, 48″ tall. This artist uses soft fiberforms. "I've worked with the historic combination of lashed reed and felt, the secure barrier of the nomads. As a woodworker and weaver, this union of materials furthers my search for an androgynous form." Photographer, Harriet Hartigan.

above right: Secrets by Sas Colby. 6″ wide, 6″ tall, 3″ deep. "Each compartment of this box of padded silk over cardboard construction holds a small book printed with rubber stamps. A silken cord winds from glass beads to a glass ring to secure the secrets."

below left: Cornucopia by Arlene Pitlik. 3′ wide, 30″ tall, 18″ deep. By knotting and wrapping wool, rayon and welt cords the artist expresses "plant life bursting from a protective cocoon." Photographer, Mark Gooby.

below right: Ode to the Wreck and Creation Womb by Joan Michaels-Paque. 18″ wide, 18″ tall, 6″ deep. This piece uses the artist's penetrating planes concept and principles innate to math, science, and art. Photographer, Henry P. Paque.

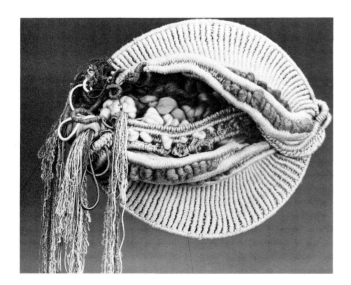

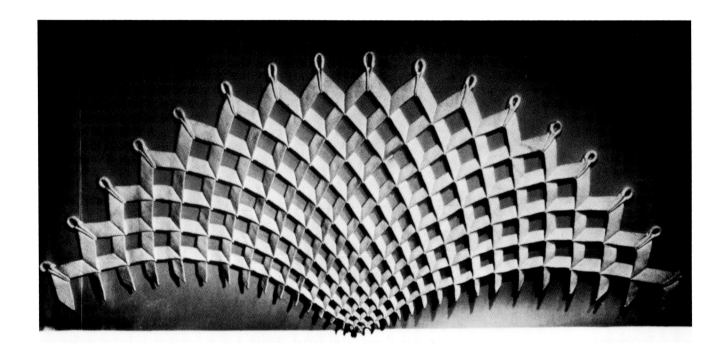

above: Increments by Joan Michaels-Paque. 18′ wide, 6′ 6″ tall, 5″
deep. This artist has found a gold mine of creativity based on her
"interest in the growth and acceleration principles in math/art/
science." In this *Progression series* pieces are self-sustaining (support
themselves without an armature). Photographer, Henry P. Paque.

Slot Machine by Joan Arrizabalaga. 15″ wide, 18″ high, 14″ deep.
Beautifully sewn seams and humorously accurate patterns for parts
create a beguiling slot machine that reveals the remarkable skill of the
artist in this medium.

Conclusion

Soft sculpture brings pleasure to those who make it and
others who see it. People who make it delight in manipulating flexible materials to create magical figures.
They appreciate that, as a general rule, there is little of the
smell, dirt, heavy labor, and major expense of some
media.

Soft sculpture reaches the public in many ways. Many
forms are appreciated exclusively as art, others as toys or
educational aids for children or for businesses. Soft
sculpture enriches other arts such as *wearable art —*
ballet or masquerade costumes. Size of soft sculpture can
range from enormous — a hot air balloon to ride in or a
stuffed parade float, to miniscule — a small ornament or
a piece of jewelry. Such versatility displays the active
imagination of its artists.

Egyptian Wing by Sally Cooley Hammerman. 36″ wide, 35″ tall, 3″ thick. "My problem is how to transfer the beautiful forms and concepts of Egyptian art into 'soft art.' I stitched and stuffed individual feather shapes, some with welted edges, then overlayed them to make the wing." Photographer, Sally Cooley Hammerman.

below left: Paul Revere by Susan Bird Kittredge. 15″ wide, 19″ tall. Nineteen similar soft sculpture pieces appeared in color as divider pages for *Effective English* Grade 5. These illustrations are machine sewn fabric collage and polyester stuffed soft sculpture. Pieces were photographed at the publishers. Reproduced by permission of the Silver Burdett Company, c. 1979.

below right: Flamingo Cape by Lynn DiNino. Life-sized. "This floor length cape is fully lined, with a detachable neck piece (the pair of flamingos riding on your neck) otherwise known as 'you'll never walk alone.' " It is currently on tour in a show called Traveling Modes and Devices, featured at the Western Associations of Museums. Photographer, Donn Leber.

Bibliography

SOFT SCULPTURE

Hall, Carolyn Vosburg. *Stitched and Stuffed Art.* New York: Doubleday and Co., 1973.

Meilach, Dona. *Soft Sculpture and Other Soft Art Forms.* New York: Crown Publishers, 1974.

Rose, Barbara. *Claes Oldenburg.* Boston: New York Graphics Society, 1970.

ART AND DESIGN

Guyler, Vivian Varney. *Design in Nature.* Worcester, Massachusetts: Davis Publications.

Lucie-Smith, Edward. *Art Now, From Abstract Expressionism to Super Realism.* New York: William Morrow, 1977.

Moholy-Nagy, Laszlo. *Vision in Motion.* Chicago: Paul Theobald and Co., 1947.

METHODS AND MATERIALS

Bartley, Regina. *The Joy of Machine Embroidery.* South Bend, Indiana: Regnery/ Gateway, 1976.

Belfer, Nancy. *Designing and Stitching in Appliqué.* Worcester, Massachusetts: Davis Publications, 1972.

————. *Designing in Batik and Tie Dye.* Worcester, Massachusetts: Davis Publications, 1972.

Coats and Clark. *Coats and Clark's Sewing Book.* Racine, Wisconsin: Golden Press, 1976.

Creager, Clara. *Weaving: A Creative Approach for Beginners.* New York: Doubleday and Co., 1974.

Gordon, Beverly. *Felt Making.* New York: Watson-Guptill Publications, 1980.

Gorsline, Douglas. *What People Wore.* New York: Bonanza Books, Crown Publishers, 1952.

Guild, Vera. *Painting With Stitches.* Worcester, Massachusetts: Davis Publications, 1976.

Hall, Carolyn Vosburg. *The Sewing Machine Craft Book.* New York: Van Nostrand Reinhold Co., 1980.

Harvey, Virginia. *Macramé: The Art of Knotting.* New York: Van Nostrand Reinhold Co., 1976.

Kaufman, Glen and Johnson, Meda. *Design on Fabric.* New York: Van Nostrand Reinhold Co., 1976.

Kleeburg, Irene, ed. *The Butterick Fabric Handbook.* New York: Butterick, 1975.

Larsen, Jack L. and Buhler, Alfred. *The Dyer's Art.* New York: Van Nostrand Reinhold Company, 1977.

Laurie, Jean R. and Law, Ruth. *Hand Made Toys and Games.* New York: Doubleday and Co., 1975.

Martens, Rachel. *Modern Patchwork.* New York: Doubleday and Co., 1971.

Meilach, Dona. *Batik and Tie Dye.* New York: Crown Publishers, 1973.

Michaels-Paque, Joan. *A Creative and Conceptual Analysis of Textiles.* 4455 N. Frederick Avenue, Shorewood, Wisconsin: Joan Michaels-Paque, 1978.

Phillips, Mary W. *Knitting.* New York: Watts, 1977.

————. *Knitting, Step-by-Step.* Racine, Wisconsin, Golden Press, 1968.

Rainey, Sarita. *Fiber Expressions: Knotting and Looping.* Worcester, Massachusetts: Davis Publications, 1979.

Robinson, Sharon. *Contemporary Basketry.* Worcester, Massachusetts: Davis Publications, 1978.

Schwalbach, Mathilda V. and James A. *Screen Process Printing for Serigraphers and Textile Designers.* New York: Van Nostrand Reinhold Co. 1970.

Stafford, Carleton, and Bishop, Robert. *America's Quilts and Coverlets.* New York: E. P. Dutton, 1972.

The Art of Sewing Series. Alexandria, Virginia: Time-Life Books, 1974. Tricot, Mon, ed. *Knitting Dictionary, 900 Stitches and Patterns.* New York: Crown Publishers, 1971.

PERIODICALS

Fiberarts Magazine. 50 College Street, Asheville, NC 28801.

American Crafts (Formerly Craft Horizons). 22 West 55th Street, New York, NY 10019.

left: Skyhawk by the author. 24" long. Commissioned by Buick to promote Skyhawk cars, this bird contained a small speaker in his chest, and springs were attached to solenoid batteries in his legs. He could wobble back and forth from his perch on the display stand and respond to the "pitchman's" questions. Owner, Buick.

Glossary

acetate a synthetic filament, yarn, or fabric made from cellulose (wood or plant material), and stronger than viscose rayon.

appliqué a French word meaning to apply a fabric patch to a background fabric by sewing.

batik a fabric dyeing technique in which wax applied to fabric resists dyeing in those areas.

batt, batting an even layer of stuffing fibers in cotton, wool or polyester fiberfill, available in quilting or upholstry sizes and thicknesses.

bias a diagonal fold or cut across woven fabric which allows for the most stretching or easing.

bodkin a long narrow tool used for threading yarn or elastic through a casing.

bonded batting a layer of fibers of even thickness (cotton, wool or polyester fibers) in which fibers are adhered together to prevent shifting or pulling apart.

coiling a basketry technique for shaping a continuous strand into a three dimensional shape. Each succeeding coil is wrapped or sewn to the previous adjacent coil.

couching a method of sewing a laid-on thread, yarn or cord to a background fabric by using small hand or machine stitching. It is used when the laid-on fiber is too large, fragile or loosely spun to stitch.

crewel an embroidery technique using wool yarns to sew decorative patterns on a loosely woven background.

cross grain the widthwise yarns in a woven fabric.

dart a shaped tuck sewn in fabric for contouring.

diameter the widest distance across a circle, tube or ball.

dimensional stability the firmness of a fabric and its ability to resist pulling or sagging.

ease a technique of shortening or adding fullness to fabric by gathering slightly on a basting thread.

embroidery 1. a hand sewing technique for embellishing fabric by using embroidery or tapestry needles and decorative threads, i.e. crewel, needlepoint, etc. 2. a machine sewn technique for decorating fabric using sewing threads or machine embroidery threads, done by free-motion, satin stitch (zigzag stitching) couching or other means.

felting a technique for making wool fabric by matting fibers by using heat, moisture, pressure and movement.

fiber any flexible material that is 100 times as long as it is wide and possesses the qualities for making yarns and fabrics: spinnability, strength, dyeability, etc.

finish surface qualities applied to fabrics for special effects.

free motion embroidery a means of stitching in any direction with a sewing machine by releasing the feed mechanism, or using the darning foot attachment, then guiding the fabric using one's hands as hoops.

French knot an embroidery stitch formed by winding thread around the needle on the fabric surface then pulling it into a knot from the reverse side.

French seam a seam with no raw edges, made by seaming on the face side of fabric, turning, then seaming on the reverse side.

grain the lengthwise or warp direction of fibers in woven fabric. Fabric may shrink in this direction due to stretching in the weaving process.

gusset an inset piece of fabric added to reduce stress on corners.

hand the feel of fabric. Dyed fabric has a more natural hand than fabric thickened in spots by textile paint.

ikat a dye technique in which certain predetermined sections of the warp yarns are tightly bound to resist the dye. This is done prior to weaving.

laminating a process of adhering layers of fabric together by heat fusion, adhesive or stitching.

mordant a substance used in dyeing to fix the coloring matter.

mylar a plastic sheeting, colored or clear, that can be cut and sewn like fabric.

photo silk screen a process used to print designs on fabric (or other materials) in which the stencil is made by exposing a positive image onto a light sensitive gel.

pi a symbol π denoting the ratio of the circumference of a circle to its diameter, used to compute the measurement of circles, tubes and balls. The ratio has a value of 3.14 +.

polyester a strong synthetic fiber made from petroleum, used for stuffing, thread, fabrics and combining with other fibers.

presser foot a sewing machine part that holds the fabric onto the machine while the stitch is formed. It comes in many shapes for different tasks: darning, hemming, embroidering, etc.

procion dye a dye that reacts or combines with the fiber for brighter more permanent color.

quilting 1. a method of sewing face, filler and backing fabric layers together to make quilting. 2. a stitched line in layered fabrics that quilts the layers together and forms a dimensional padded surface.

radius the distance from the center of a circle to the rim used (with pi) to compute the dimensions.

selvedge the edge of a fabric woven or taped so it will not ravel.

trapunto a quilting technique in which certain areas receive additional padding for a bas relief effect.

turn means to seam two pieces of fabric, then turn the piece to the other side so the seams are hidden.

twining the earliest means of entwining, or twisting, fibers to create larger objects, used to make nets, baskets, etc.

warp and weft weaving terms indicating the direction of the threads. Warp threads wound on the loom run the length of the fabric and must be strong enough to resist the wear of the weaving process. Weft (or filler) threads are interwoven across the warp threads.

welt seam a double sewn seam for added strength.

wrapping a technique used to add to the size, color or strength of a core yarn by winding added yarn around one or more core yarns.

yarn 1. a cord spun from wool or other fibers used for knitting, crochet, weaving or other fiber techniques. 2. a term used in industry to mean any thread, yarn or cord used to weave or knit a fabric.

zigzag a sewing machine stitch formed by the sideways swing of the needle.

Acknowledgments

Crafts books thrive and grow from the vitality of the field they represent. The contemporary fibers movement has burst forth with imaginative soft sculptures skillfully made by artists from all parts of the country. My warm thanks to the 150 who contributed so many fine slides and photographs, many of which I did not have space to include. Several wrote letters sharing their ideas on technique, getting started, work spaces, selling works, the state of the art, and other problems and pleasures. I quoted as many as possible so the reader could meet these delightful "soft" artists too. Thanks also to The Works Gallery in Philadelphia, and Fiber Arts Magazine for help in locating fiber artists. Special thanks to my current apprentice, Gail Molnar, for her invaluable help. Thanks to Rosemary Squires, Pat McLaughlin, and Shirley Gould for assistance with organizational challenges.

Carolyn Vosburg Hall, 1980